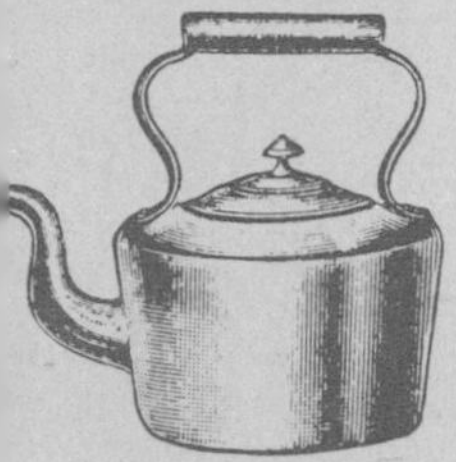

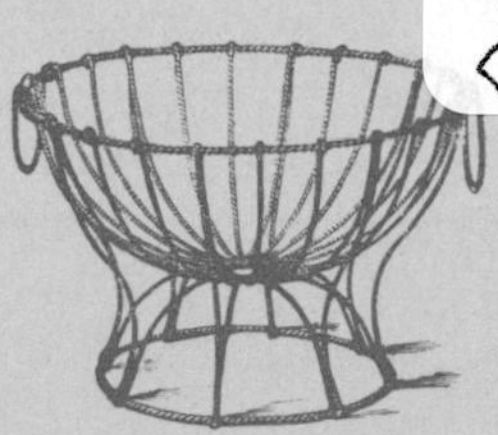

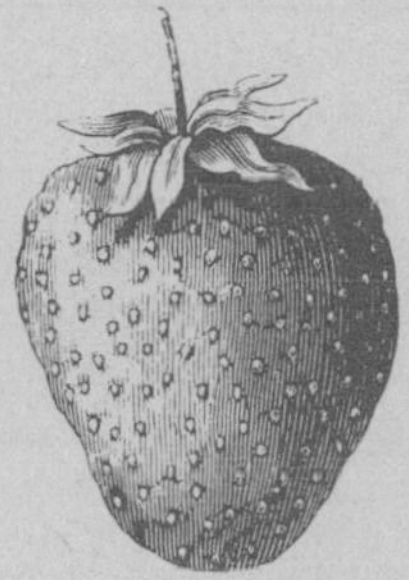

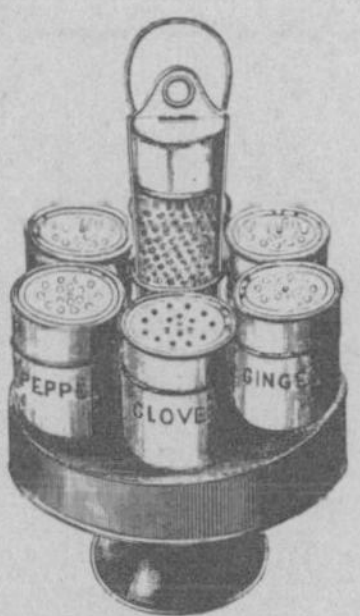
CLOVES

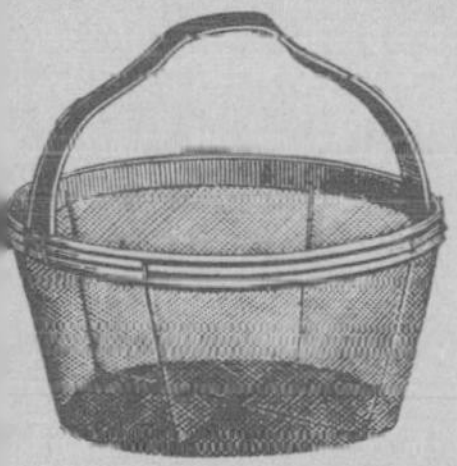

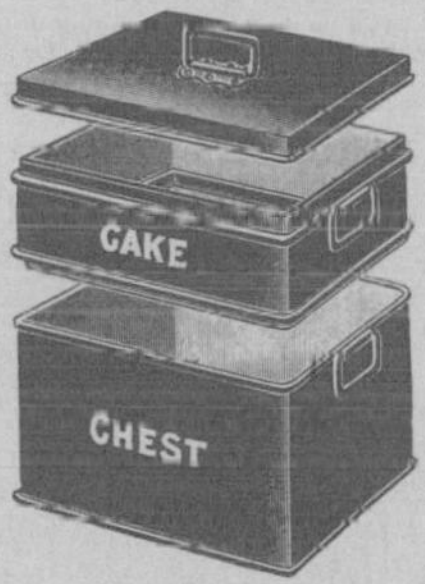
CAKE
CHEST

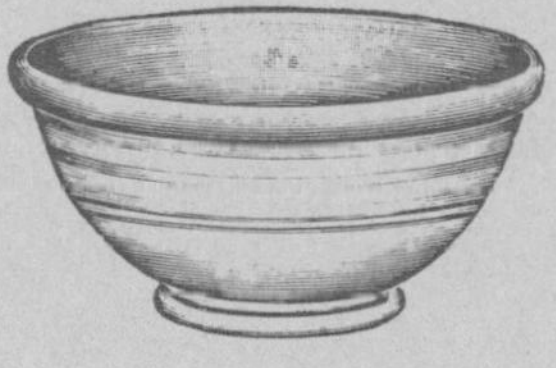

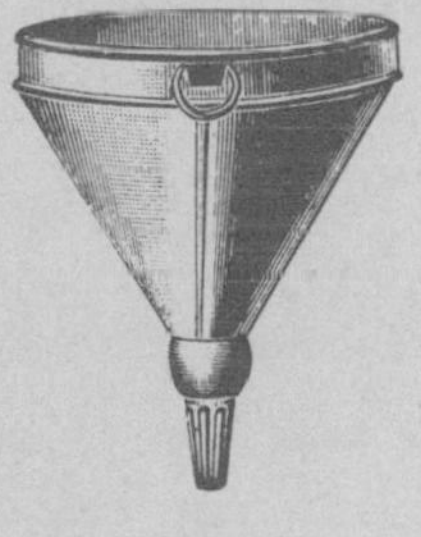

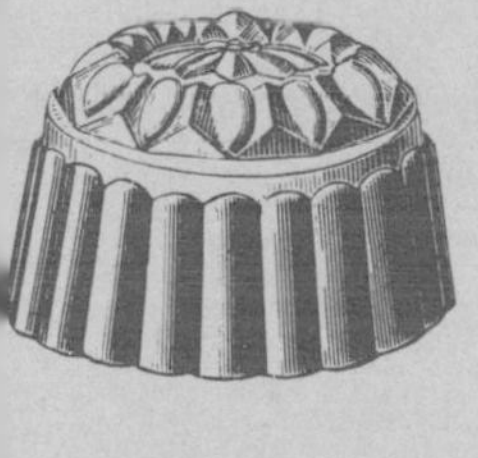

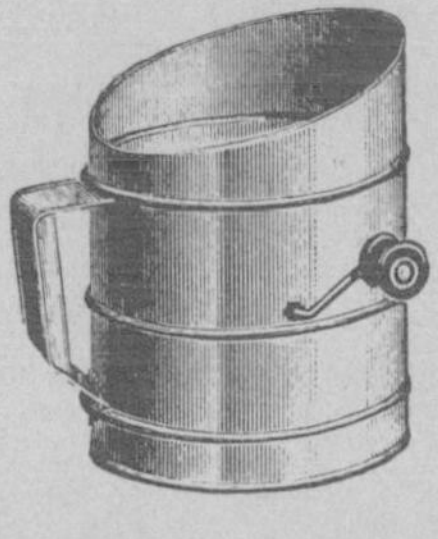

Southern Living.

The SOUTHERN HERITAGE COOKBOOK LIBRARY

The SOUTHERN HERITAGE
Pies
and
Pastry
COOKBOOK

OXMOOR HOUSE
Birmingham, Alabama

Southern Living.

The Southern Heritage Cookbook Library

The Southern Heritage PIES AND PASTRY Cookbook

Manager, Editorial Projects: Ann H. Harvey
Southern Living® *Foods Editor*: Jean W. Liles
Production Editor: Joan E. Denman
Foods Editor: Katherine M. Eakin
Director, Test Kitchen: Laura N. Nestelroad
Test Kitchen Home Economists: Pattie B. Booker, Kay E. Clarke,
    Marilyn Hannan, Elizabeth J. Taliaferro
Production Manager: Jerry R. Higdon
Copy Editor: Melinda E. West
Editorial Assistants: Mary Ann Laurens, Karen P. Traccarella
Food Photographer: Jim Bathie
Food Stylist: Sara Jane Ball
Layout Designer: Christian von Rosenvinge
Mechanical Artist: Faith Nance
Research Editor: Janice Randall
Research Assistant: Evelyn deFrees

Special Consultants

Art Director: Irwin Glusker
Heritage Consultant: Meryle Evans
Foods Writer: Lillian B. Marshall
Food and Recipe Consultants: Marilyn Wyrick Ingram,
    Audrey P. Stehle

Cover (clockwise from front): Alabama Pecan Pie (page 52), Lime and Lemon Chiffon Tarts (page 118), Coconut Meringue Pie (page 95), Peach Cobbler Supreme (page 40). Photograph by Jim Bathie.

CONTENTS

Introduction   7

Easy as Pie   11
Pastries and Meringues

Pick of the Crop   27
Fruit and Berry Pies

Our Native Harvest   51
Nut and Vegetable Pies

Old-World Heritage   65
Custard, Chess, and Cheese Pies

Pride of the Cook   87
Cream Pies, Plain and Fancy

Chill to Set   103
Chiffon and Icebox Pies

Teatime Treats   115
Tarts and Tartlets

Little Pastries   127
Dumplings, Fried Pies, and Turnovers

Acknowledgments   138   Index   140

INTRODUCTION

The stout British "pye," ennobled in literature by such as Chaucer, Shakespeare, and Dickens, was a savory meat mixture swathed in a thick, heavy dough. It could contain larks, for example, or mutton, or veal and ham, or steak and kidney, and it could be served hot or cold. Small meat pies called pasties were made to be eaten out of the hand. An early sort of sandwich, the pasty went to the coal mines and to the fields to furnish the laborer with a nourishing lunch.

Tarts, as differentiated from pies, were sweet and were baked in a much lighter crust. They were served at any time during the meal, not necessarily for dessert; meals were most likely to end with cheese or a savoury. Meats were not safe from sweetening, as witness the venerable mincemeat pie.

Once in America, the English cook (confronted by a somewhat different set of ingredients) continued to bake meat and game pies, although the meat could be and was, on occasion, bear or squirrel. It will be recalled that it was some years before the settlers' supply of domestic animals was assured. Unfamiliar nuts, fruits, and berries lent themselves to tarts, and sweetening ran to honey, molasses, and, further north, to maple sugar and syrup, until sugar became generally available.

By Martha Washington's day, the distinction between pies and tarts had begun to fade; people began to use the terms interchangeably to mean sweet pastries. Mrs. Washington's own cookbook reflects the gradual Americanization of pastries: The old English recipes were kept, not only for mincemeat pie, but for tarts made of sweetened lettuce, parsnips . . . even a Tart of Hipps, requiring a quart of rose hips, the fruit of the rose. But apple pie was here as well.

The evolution of the American pie as we know it, with a crust on the bottom and variously topped, would appear to have been slightly more of a Southern development than otherwise. Eliza Leslie, writing her *New Cookery Book* (1857) in Philadelphia, opined that "Except in very plain country places a fruit pie with two crusts (under and upper) is now seen but rarely." Her method was to place only a border of puff pastry on the rim of the plate, bake it, pour in cooked filling, and sift sugar over it.

Miss Leslie, it may be inferred, had not had the pleasure of visiting a contemporary food writer named Mary Randolph in her anything-but-plain circumstances in Virginia. Independently, Randolph was working toward an American way of cooking American ingredients. In *The Virginia Housewife*, 1824, she offered an apple pie with crusts (under and upper) while remaining British in calling many of her pies puddings, as in ". . . stir it over the fire to thicken it, pour it into a paste and bake it."

By 1876, Mary Frances Henderson, writing in St. Louis, dared to say in her *Practical Cooking and Dinner Giving* that "in England, only an upper crust is made. In this country there is generally only an under crust, with bars of paste crossed over the top. I prefer this mode. . . ."

Marion Cabell Tyree, writing about the same time in *Housekeeping in Old Virginia*, used the term tart only for small, one-serving pastries as we do now. Her recipes for Tyler Pudding and Irish Potato Pudding end with the instruction "Bake in a paste," which turned her pudding into American pie. She simply had not shaken the English habit of calling a dessert a pudding. Tyree's puddings were mostly pies, then. But she included a section called pies, with many of the recipes calling for a topping of meringue, a mechanism, it appears, for distinguishing a pudding from a pie. Because there were few ovens in colonial days, many of these early recipes permitted a pudding to be either steamed in a dampened and floured cloth or, less frequently, baked in a "paste."

The colonists' brand new supermarket of ingredients with which to fill their pudding bowls called forth the cook's inventiveness. Watching the Indians sweeten nuts, berries, or pumpkin with honey gave them enough for a start. Hickory and black walnuts were abundant in the fall, as were chestnuts. There are early recipes for native nuts in puddings, but it was not until after the Civil War, when the pecan began to flourish across the Southern states, that the pie most associated with the warmer tier of states was born. The variations are legion, as demonstrated by the wide swing from, say, the maple syrup version from the Wayside Inn in Virginia to the Tupelo Honey Pecan Pie from Florida which utilizes honey made from the nectar of the tupelo tree. The peanut, after a long detour from Peru to Italy to Africa to North America, became the basis for another typical Southern pie.

Native pumpkins and squashes were reliable pie

fillings year-round, as they could be dried and reconstituted. Add sweet potatoes and white ones, tomatoes both green and ripe. Bean Pie? An Oklahoman whose parents were married in Indian Territory remembers it well: Her mother also ". . . made pies from vinegar, sheep sorrel, green grapes . . . even carrots." These were just a few of the "poor man's pies" made by people trying to eat well while scrabbling homes out of inhospitable wildernesses.

In addition to tarts and pastries containing beans, pears, apples, and quinces in a sixteenth-century menu by Bartolomeo Scappi, chef to Pope Pius V, there is mention of "large pies filled with custard cream." Custard pies are hardly news anymore, but they've been embroidered upon by Southern cooks who have added things like chocolate, coconut, and so on, barely keeping the principle of egg for thickening.

Perfectionism peaks when the Southern baker surveys a cream pie with a lightly swirled and browned meringue, slices it carefully with a wet knife, and finds that the filling holds its shape at room temperature.

"Chill until set. . . ." How familiar the term! Yet, chronologically, pies that "bake" in the refrigerator are our youngest heritage entry in the nine-inch pie category. While ice and iceboxes were undoubtedly utilized before the advent of electric refrigeration, the chill-and-set pie came into its own in the 1920s.

Among our sweet delights, let's save room for those little fried, boiled, or baked morsels many of us would choose over the grandest meringue or the richest chess pie. Dumplings, fried pies, turnovers: all have an assigned place in our ancestral recipe books, and they have lost none of their charm.

Thinking small again, consider the tart as we now use the term after the fashion of Marion Cabell Tyree, and the tiny, bite-size tartlet or tassie that we see at parties and, if given the opportunity, eat of too freely! As to the name "tassie," a fair guess: An anonymous culprit converted the Scottish word for a wee drinkie into a wee nibble.

While our pies have evolved away from the English "pyes," we may still thank those colonists for the infamous Southern sweet tooth, echoing that old admonition from the loving mother to a restive child: "'Ave a sweet, dearie." Sweets make us happy.

While there is nothing so American as apple pie, there is nothing more Southern than pie of any kind.

EASY AS PIE

Pastries and Meringues

W hen Thomas Jefferson put quill to paper to write the Declaration of Independence, nothing could have been further from his mind than pastry. But one of the benefits of America's distancing from England was the chance for our pastries to evolve away from the heavy, thick sorts made of suet or lard or "drippings" dissolved in hot water. Composed of one part fat to two parts flour, this dough was tough because "pyes" were sometimes baked in free-standing (raised) shells that had been formed around a wooden bowl. Hearty meat filling would have broken a tender crust.

The other extreme in pastry is puff paste. Of course the English had it from the French, who, for all we know, probably got it from the Romans. Puff paste is made from two parts flour to at least one part butter; professional pastry chefs can work with equal weights of flour and butter. So how can puff contain up to twice as much fat without being twice as tough and heavy?

It is in the construction: The old suet or hot water pastry was mixed to a homogenous mass and kneaded to activate the gluten in the flour, causing the dough to toughen. In puff pastry, layers of firm butter are rolled between layers of flour paste with a minimum of handling. In the oven, steam forms and forces the layers apart, forming pockets of air that separate the gossamer flakes.

Mary Randolph and other nineteenth-century food writers called for puff paste as though it were as handy as packaged pie shells are now. Their recipes were admirably succinct; modern recipes are more detailed, but one must not be put off by the sheer length of a recipe. Many good things take almost as long to read as to cook.

We may choose from pastries and toppings unknown in previous centuries. Jefferson served meringue glacé at Monticello, but there is little evidence of soft meringue toppings being used widely until the late 1800s. Mrs. Randolph came close when she put frothed egg white on one pudding, dredged it with sugar, and browned it with a salamander.

Here are our earliest pastries as well as later creations.

Many kinds of pastry can be envisioned in this array of ingredients: Flour-based shells, with or without egg, as well as coconut crust and those made of cracker and cookie crumbs.

PASTRIES

PASTRY MIX

7 cups all-purpose flour
1 tablespoon salt
2 cups shortening

Combine flour and salt in a large mixing bowl; cut in shortening with a pastry blender until mixture resembles coarse meal. Place pastry mix in a covered container, and store in refrigerator for up to 1 month. Yield: pastry mix for seven 9-inch pastry shells.

Single-Crust Pastry Shell:

1¾ cups Pastry Mix
4 to 5 tablespoons cold water

Sprinkle water evenly over pastry mix. Stir with a fork until dry ingredients are moistened. Shape dough into a ball; chill. Yield: pastry for one 9-inch pie.

Refer to pages 14 and 15 for step-by-step instructions for preparing a baked or unbaked pastry shell.

BASIC DOUBLE-CRUST PASTRY

2 cups all-purpose flour
½ teaspoon salt
¾ cup shortening
5 to 6 tablespoons cold water

Combine flour and salt in a medium mixing bowl; cut in shortening with a pastry blender until mixture resembles coarse meal. Sprinkle water evenly over surface; stir with a fork until dry ingredients are moistened. Shape dough into a ball; chill.

Roll half of pastry to ⅛-inch thickness on a lightly floured surface; fit into a 9-inch pieplate leaving a ½-inch overhang.

Add filling as directed in desired recipe. Trim off overhanging edges.

Roll remaining pastry into an 11-inch circle. Moisten the edge of the bottom pastry with water.

Fit top pastry over filling. Trim edge of top pastry, leaving a ½-inch overhang. Fold overhang under edge of bottom pastry, pressing firmly to seal; flute. Cut slits in top crust to allow steam to escape. Bake as directed in desired recipe. Yield: pastry for one 9-inch double-crust or lattice-top pie.

Lattice-Top Pastry:

Roll half of pastry to ⅛-inch thickness on a lightly floured surface; fit into a 9-inch pieplate, leaving a ¾-inch overhang. Add filling as directed in desired recipe. Do not trim overhanging edges.

Roll remaining pastry to an 11-inch circle. Cut into ½-inch strips. Moisten edge of bottom pastry with water. Lay half of strips across filling, spacing them about ¾-inch apart. Repeat procedure with remaining strips, arranging in the opposite direction. Press strips to edge of bottom pastry and trim even with overhanging edge of bottom pastry. Fold the ¾-inch overhang and pastry strips under, pressing firmly so edge of pastry is even with rim of pieplate. Flute as desired.

BEST LARD PASTRY

3 cups all-purpose flour
1 teaspoon salt
1 cup lard
¼ cup plus 1 tablespoon milk
1 egg
1 tablespoon vinegar

Combine flour and salt in a large bowl. Cut in lard with a pastry blender until mixture resembles coarse meal. Combine last 3 ingredients; add to flour mixture. Stir with a fork until dry ingredients are moistened. Shape dough into a ball; chill. Use as directed in desired recipe. Yield: pastry for one 10-inch deep-dish double-crust pie.

BASIC BUTTER PASTRY

1 cup all-purpose flour
¼ teaspoon salt
½ cup butter, chilled
3 to 4 tablespoons cold water

Combine flour and salt in a small bowl; cut in butter with a pastry blender until mixture resembles coarse meal. Sprinkle water evenly over surface; stir with a fork until dry ingredients are moistened. Shape dough into a ball; chill. Use as directed in desired recipe. Yield: pastry for one 9-inch pie.

QUANTITY PASTRY

4 cups all-purpose flour
1¼ cups butter or margarine
¾ cup cold milk
1 egg

Place flour in a large mixing bowl; cut in butter with a pastry blender until mixture resembles coarse meal. Combine milk and egg; add to flour mixture. Stir with a fork until dry ingredients are moistened. Shape dough into a ball; chill. Use as directed in desired recipe. Yield: pastry for four 9-inch pies.

"SHORT" PASTRY

3 cups all-purpose flour
½ teaspoon salt
¼ cup shortening
5 tablespoons cold water
1 egg, beaten
1 teaspoon vinegar

Combine flour and salt in a large bowl; cut in shortening with a pastry blender until mixture resembles coarse meal. Combine water, egg, and vinegar; add to flour mixture. Stir with a fork until dry ingredients are moistened. Shape dough into a ball; chill. Use as directed in desired recipe. Yield: pastry for one 9-inch double-crust pie.

BASIC PASTRY HOW-TO

BASIC PASTRY

1 cup all-purpose flour
¼ teaspoon salt
¼ cup plus 2 tablespoons
   shortening
2 to 3 tablespoons cold water

Combine flour and salt in a small mixing bowl; cut in shortening with a pastry blender until mixture resembles coarse meal. Sprinkle water evenly over surface of flour mixture; stir with a fork until dry ingredients are moistened. Shape dough into a ball; chill. Use as directed in desired recipe. Yield: pastry for one 9-inch pie.

Step 1 — Combine flour and salt in a small mixing bowl; cut in shortening with a pastry blender until mixture resembles coarse meal.

Step 4 — Place dough in center of a lightly floured surface or pastry cloth. Using a floured rolling pin, roll dough with light even strokes from the center of the dough to the edge. Roll into a circle ⅛-inch thick.

Step 5 — Roll pastry onto rolling pin. Unroll pastry into a 9-inch pieplate being careful not to stretch the pastry.

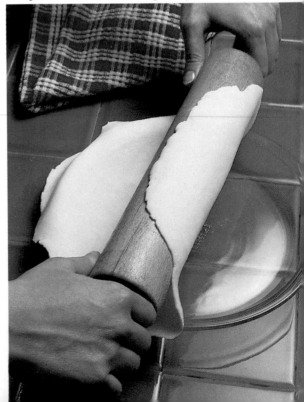

Step 2 — Sprinkle cold water evenly over surface of flour mixture. Stir with a fork until dry ingredients are moistened, being careful not to overmix.

Step 3 — Shape dough into a ball. Cover and chill.

Step 6 — Using a sharp knife or kitchen shears, trim the pastry to ½ inch beyond edge of pieplate. Fold under ½ inch of pastry to reinforce the edge. Press dough with fingers to flute as shown in picture.

Step 7 — To bake a pastry shell without filling: prick bottom and sides of pastry shell with tines of a fork. To bake a pastry shell with filling: do not prick pastry shell before filling.

DEEP-DISH PASTRY

2½ cups all-purpose flour
2 teaspoons sugar
¼ teaspoon baking powder
¼ teaspoon salt
¾ cup shortening
1 egg yolk, beaten
Water

Combine flour, sugar, baking powder, and salt; cut in shortening with a pastry blender until mixture resembles coarse meal. Combine egg yolk and water to equal 1 cup. Add liquid to flour mixture; stir with a fork until dry ingredients are moistened. Shape dough into a ball; chill. Use as directed in desired recipe. Yield: pastry for one 10-inch deep-dish double-crust pie.

Note: This recipe may be used to prepare a 10-inch deep-dish bottom crust pastry with a lattice top.

CHEDDAR CHEESE PASTRY

2 cups all-purpose flour
½ teaspoon salt
Dash of red pepper
⅔ cup lard
½ cup (2 ounces) shredded sharp Cheddar cheese
6 to 7 tablespoons cold water

Combine flour, salt, and pepper; cut in lard and cheese with a pastry blender until mixture resembles coarse meal. Sprinkle water evenly over surface; stir with a fork until dry ingredients are moistened. Shape dough into a ball; chill. Use as directed in desired recipe. Yield: pastry for one 10-inch deep-dish pie.

PÂTE BRISÉE SUCRÉE

3 cups all-purpose flour
¼ cup sugar
1 teaspoon salt
1 cup butter, chilled
2 egg yolks
½ cup half-and-half

Combine flour, sugar, and salt in a small mixing bowl. Cut in butter with a pastry blender until mixture resembles coarse meal. Combine egg yolks and half-and-half; add liquid to flour mixture. Stir with a fork until dry ingredients are moistened. Shape dough into a ball; chill thoroughly. Use as directed in desired recipe. Yield: pastry for eighteen 4-inch turnovers or 6 dozen 1¾-inch tart shells.

Turn-of-the-century ad for vegetable shortening, marketed after Dr. Wesson proved that cottonseed products were edible.

Collection of Business Ame[ricana]

DR. DAVID WESSON'S STIR 'N' ROLL PASTRY SHELL

1¼ cups all-purpose flour
½ teaspoon salt
⅓ cup plus 1 tablespoon vegetable oil
2 tablespoons cold milk

Combine flour and salt in a small mixing bowl; mix well. Combine oil and milk; add to flour mixture. Stir with a fork until dry ingredients are moistened. Shape dough into a ball. Chill.

Roll dough to ⅛-inch thickness between two sheets of waxed paper. Remove top sheet of waxed paper; discard. Invert pastry, and place in a 9-inch pieplate. Remove remaining waxed paper. Trim excess pastry around edges. Fold edges under, and flute. Prick bottom and sides of shell with a fork. Bake at 475° for 8 minutes or until golden brown. Yield: one 9-inch pastry shell.

In the year 1899, the Southern Cotton Oil Company of Savannah employed Dr. David Wesson as plant chemist. It didn't take Dr. Wesson long to prove the nutritional value of cottonseed's chief by-product; edible oil and other shortenings hit the market about 1900. The company developed the original stir-and-roll pie crust from the oil that bears Wesson's name. The brilliant chemist went on to utilize cottonseed soap-stock to make glycerine for World War I and pioneered the production of meat analogues and flour in the 1930s. Although his achievements were many and varied, it is his oil for which he is remembered.

PUFF PASTRY RECIPE

PUFF PASTE

1 cup butter
1½ cups all-purpose flour
½ cup sifted cake flour
¼ teaspoon salt
¾ cup cold water

Let butter stand at room temperature 15 minutes. Set 2 tablespoons of butter aside. Place remaining butter between two pieces of lightly floured waxed paper. Pound with a rolling pin to make butter pliable. (Butter should become the consistency of firm dough.) As butter flattens, use a small spatula to shape butter into a 5-inch square with slightly rounded edges. Wrap in plastic wrap. Refrigerate while making dough.

Combine flour and salt in a bowl. Work reserved 2 tablespoons butter into flour by rubbing together between the fingers. Add water; stir with a fork until dry ingredients are moistened. Turn dough onto a lightly floured surface; knead 30 times. Cover by inverting bowl over dough. Let rest 10 minutes.

Lightly flour a smooth surface. Roll dough to an 8-inch circle. Mark a 6-inch square within circle of dough. Roll each side of square until dough resembles a flower with 4 petals. (Center of dough will be thick.)

Place chilled butter square on center square of dough. Fold dough over butter, one side at a time, bringing edges to center and overlapping slightly. Wrap in plastic wrap, and refrigerate 15 minutes.

Lightly flour surface, and add flour as necessary during following procedure. Place dough, flat side down, on surface. Press rolling pin firmly on dough 7 times, once in center and 3 times above and below center to flatten dough and seal edges. Roll dough into a 14- x 6-inch rectangle, keeping thickness of dough as even as possible, and corners square.

Fold dough in thirds to resemble a folded letter. Give dough a quarter turn to the right. Press with rolling pin to seal edges. Repeat rolling and folding procedure, and refrigerate 15 minutes.

Repeat rolling and folding procedure 4 additional times, refrigerating dough for 15 minutes after every two turns. Dough will be rolled and folded a total of 6 turns. Refrigerate 15 minutes or longer before using in a recipe. Yield: 2 cups puff paste.

Note: Puff paste may be refrigerated for 3 days or frozen for 3 months. If refrigerated longer than 30 minutes, allow puff paste to stand at room temperature 5 minutes before rolling out or 30 minutes if frozen.

Step 1 — Place butter between two pieces of lightly floured waxed paper. Pound with a rolling pin to make butter pliable. Use a small spatula to shape butter into a 5-inch square. Wrap in plastic wrap. Refrigerate while making dough.

Step 4 — Place chilled butter square on center square of dough. Fold dough over butter, one side at a time, bringing edges to center and overlapping slightly to completely cover butter square. Wrap in plastic wrap, and refrigerate 15 minutes.

Step 2 — Combine flour and salt. Work 2 tablespoons butter into flour by rubbing together between fingers. Add water; stir with a fork until moistened. Turn dough onto a lightly floured surface; knead 30 times. Cover; let rest 10 minutes.

Step 3 — Roll dough on a lightly floured surface into an 8-inch circle. Mark a 6-inch square within circle of dough. Roll out each side of square until dough resembles a flower with 4 petals. (Center of dough will be thick.)

Step 5 — Place dough, flat side down, on a lightly floured surface. Press rolling pin firmly into dough to flatten dough and seal edges. Roll flattened dough into a 14- x 6-inch rectangle. Fold dough in thirds to resemble a folded letter.

Step 6 — Press edges to seal. Give dough a quarter turn to the right. Roll dough into a 14- x 6-inch rectangle and fold in thirds. Refrigerate 15 minutes. Repeat rolling and folding procedure four additional times; chill 15 minutes after every two turns.

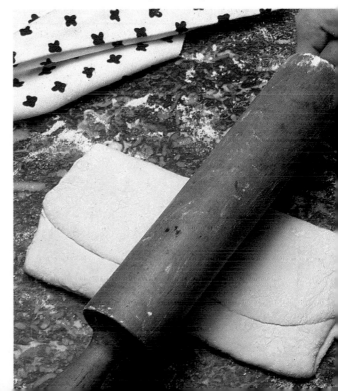

Pies

CREAM CHEESE PASTRY SHELL

½ cup butter or margarine, softened
1 (3-ounce) package cream cheese, softened
1 cup all-purpose flour
⅛ teaspoon salt

Combine butter and cream cheese; cream until smooth. Add flour and salt, mixing well. Shape dough into a ball; chill at least 2 hours.

Roll dough to ⅛-inch thickness on a lightly floured surface. Place in a 9-inch pieplate; trim excess pastry around edges. Fold edge under, and flute. Prick bottom and sides of shell with a fork. Bake at 425° for 12 to 15 minutes or until pastry is golden brown. Yield: one 9-inch pastry shell.

EGG PASTRY SHELLS

3 cups all-purpose flour
1½ teaspoons salt
1 cup shortening
½ cup cold water
1 egg, slightly beaten
1 teaspoon vinegar

Combine flour and salt in a large mixing bowl; cut in shortening with a pastry blender until mixture resembles coarse meal. Combine water, egg, and vinegar in a small bowl. Add liquid to flour mixture; stir with a fork until dry ingredients are moistened. Shape dough into a ball; chill.

Divide dough into three equal portions. Roll each portion to ⅛-inch thickness on a lightly floured surface. Place each in a 9-inch pieplate; trim excess pastry around edges. Fold edges under, and flute. Prick bottom and sides of shell with a fork. Bake at 425° for 15 minutes or until golden brown. Yield: three 9-inch pastry shells.

ALL-PURPOSE TART SHELLS

2 cups all-purpose flour
½ teaspoon salt
⅔ cup shortening
¼ cup plus 2 tablespoons cold water

Combine flour and salt in a mixing bowl; cut in shortening with a pastry blender until mixture resembles coarse meal. Sprinkle water evenly over surface; stir with a fork until dry ingredients are moistened. Shape dough into a ball; chill. Use as directed in desired recipe.

4-inch Tart Shells:

Remove pastry from refrigerator, and divide into 6 equal portions. Roll each portion to ⅛-inch thickness on a lightly floured surface. Fit each pastry into a 4-inch tart pan. Prick bottom and sides of pastry shells with a fork. Bake at 350° for 15 minutes or until lightly browned. Yield: six 4-inch tart shells.

2¾-inch Tart Shells:

Remove pastry from refrigerator, and divide into 12 equal portions. Roll each portion to ⅛-inch thickness on a lightly floured surface. Fit each pastry into a 2¾-inch muffin tin. Prick bottom and sides of pastry shells with a fork. Bake at 475° for 7 minutes or until lightly browned. Yield: 1 dozen 2¾-inch tart shells.

1¾-inch Tart Shells:

Remove pastry from refrigerator; shape dough into forty-eight 1-inch balls. Place dough balls in lightly greased 1¾-inch muffin pans; shape each into a shell. Prick bottom and sides of pastry shells with a fork. Bake at 425° for 10 minutes or until lightly browned. Yield: 4 dozen 1¾-inch tart shells.

PECAN PASTRY SHELL

1 cup all-purpose flour
½ cup chopped pecans
¼ cup firmly packed brown sugar
½ cup butter or margarine

Place flour, pecans, sugar, and butter in a 9-inch pieplate; do not stir. Bake at 400° for 15 minutes. Stir mixture to blend well. Firmly press mixture into bottom and sides of a lightly greased 9-inch pieplate. Cool. Yield: one 9-inch pastry shell.

The pecan is a member of the hickory family, the name stemming from an Algonquian term. Whereas it is said that only squirrels have the patience and equipment to benefit from the true hickory nut, the pecan is easy pickings. The Indians ground the nuts into meal and baked a nourishing bread of it, long before the advent of pecan pies.

Sylvester Graham

GRAHAM CRACKER PIECRUST

1½ cups graham cracker
  crumbs
⅓ cup sugar
⅓ cup butter or margarine,
  melted

Combine all ingredients; mix well. Firmly press mixture into bottom and sides of a lightly greased 9-inch pieplate. Bake at 350° for 10 minutes. Cool. Yield: one 9-inch piecrust.

COCONUT-GRAHAM PIECRUST

1 cup graham cracker crumbs
1 cup flaked coconut
⅓ cup sugar
⅓ cup butter or margarine,
  melted

Combine all ingredients; mix well. Firmly press mixture into bottom and sides of a lightly greased 9-inch pieplate. Bake at 350° for 10 minutes. Cool. Yield: one 9-inch piecrust.

FILBERT-GRAHAM PIECRUST

1 cup graham cracker crumbs
½ cup finely chopped filberts
⅓ cup sugar
¼ cup plus 3 tablespoons
  butter or margarine, melted

Combine all ingredients; mix well. Firmly press mixture into bottom and sides of a lightly greased 9-inch pieplate. Bake at 350° for 10 minutes. Cool. Yield: one 9-inch piecrust.

Crumb crusts in the making.

O f all the crumb crusts in the Southern baker's repertoire, the most widely used is probably the one we make of Graham crackers, because we can't remember not having them. Thank Sylvester Graham (1794-1851), the vegetarian and reformer who developed a flour from unbolted wheat. Graham flour soon became the basis for Graham crackers; crumb crusts were not far behind. Not long after Graham cracker crust became part of the cook's repertoire, other crumb crusts began to appear. Vanilla wafers, gingersnaps, chocolate cookies . . . anything that would crumble was crumbled, buttered, and pressed into pie pans. Even dried ladyfingers and stale cake were, and are, desirable as piecrust ingredients.

"I Ata Pie" sorority members in annual pie-eating contest, c.1911.

State Photographic Archives, Tallahassee

VANILLA WAFER PIECRUST

1⅓ cups vanilla wafer
    crumbs
¼ cup sugar
¼ cup plus 2 tablespoons
    butter or margarine, melted

Combine all ingredients; mix well. Press mixture into bottom and sides of a lightly greased 9-inch pieplate. Bake at 375° for 5 minutes. Cool. Yield: one 9-inch piecrust.

CHOCOLATE WAFER PIECRUST

1½ cups chocolate wafer
    crumbs
2 tablespoons sugar
¼ cup plus 2 tablespoons
    butter or margarine, melted

Combine all ingredients; mix well. Firmly press mixture into bottom and sides of a lightly greased 9-inch pieplate. Bake at 350° for 10 minutes. Cool. Yield: one 9-inch piecrust.

GINGERSNAP PIECRUST

1½ cups gingersnap crumbs
2 tablespoons sugar
¼ cup butter or margarine,
    melted

Combine gingersnaps and sugar in a small bowl. Add butter; mix well. Press mixture into bottom and sides of a lightly greased 9-inch pieplate. Bake at 350° for 10 minutes. Cool. Yield: one 9-inch piecrust.

CORN FLAKE PIECRUST

1½ cups crushed corn flakes
¼ cup plus 2 tablespoons sugar
½ cup butter or margarine, melted

Combine corn flakes, sugar, and butter; toss until well blended. Press mixture into bottom and sides of a lightly greased 9-inch pieplate. Chill at least 1 hour. Bake at 350° for 15 minutes. Cool. Yield: one 9-inch piecrust.

COCONUT PIECRUST

2 cups flaked coconut, lightly toasted
¼ cup all-purpose flour
¼ cup butter or margarine, melted

Combine coconut, flour, and butter; mix well. Press mixture into bottom and sides of a lightly greased 9-inch pieplate. Bake at 325° for 10 minutes. Cool. Yield: one 9-inch piecrust.

ZWIEBACK PIECRUST

1½ cups zwieback crumbs
⅓ cup sifted powdered sugar
⅓ cup butter or margarine, melted

Combine all ingredients; mix well. Firmly press mixture into bottom and sides of a lightly greased 9-inch pieplate. Bake at 350° for 10 minutes. Cool. Yield: one 9-inch piecrust.

An example of early cereal package fun and games, c.1900.

Cereal lovers are never without the makings of a good crust: corn flakes, rice, and wheat flakes are a few from which we choose. But give a Southerner anything crisp enough to crumble, and it is entirely possible that he'll come up with a piecrust. Even bread, dried thoroughly in the oven, is fair game. It is similar to zwieback, which is German for "twice-baked." The amount of sugar used in a crumb crust will depend upon the sweetness of the basic crumbs, and the amount of butter needed will be dictated by their dryness. Many delicious variations are possible: add a pinch of spice, a few chopped nuts, or a handful of coconut. And when a firm crust is wanted, remember that a short bake in the oven will solidify it.

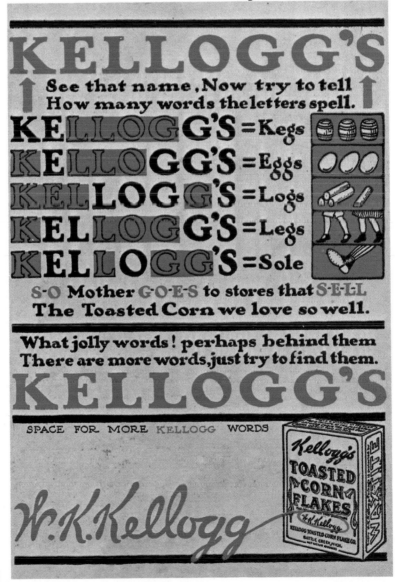

BASIC MERINGUE HOW-TO

BASIC MERINGUE

3 egg whites
½ teaspoon vanilla extract
¼ teaspoon cream of tartar
¼ cup plus 2 tablespoons sugar

Combine egg whites (at room temperature), vanilla, and cream of tartar in a medium glass or metal mixing bowl; beat until foamy. Gradually add sugar, 1 tablespoon at a time, beating until stiff peaks form and sugar dissolves.

Spread meringue over hot pie filling, carefully sealing to edge of pastry to prevent shrinkage. Bake as directed in each pie recipe. Yield: meringue for one 9-inch pie.

Note: A copper bowl is excellent for beating egg whites. The chemical reaction which occurs between the copper and egg whites helps to stabilize the mixture. Cream of tartar should be omitted when beating egg whites in a copper bowl.

Step 1 — Combine egg whites (at room temperature), vanilla, and cream of tartar in a medium glass or metal mixing bowl. (Do not use cream of tartar if using a copper bowl.) Using a large balloon whisk or electric mixer, beat egg whites 1 minute or until foamy.

Step 2 — Gradually add sugar, one tablespoon at a time, beating well after each addition. Continue beating until sugar is completely dissolved and mixture forms stiff, glossy peaks.

Step 3 — Spoon meringue over hot pie filling, spreading to edge of pie. Seal meringue to the pastry shell to prevent shrinkage during baking. Bake pie as directed in individual pie recipe.

MERINGUES

POWDERED SUGAR MERINGUE

3 egg whites
½ teaspoon cream of tartar
¼ cup plus 2 tablespoons sifted powdered sugar
½ teaspoon vanilla extract

Combine egg whites (at room temperature) and cream of tartar in a medium glass or metal mixing bowl; beat until foamy. Gradually add sugar, 1 tablespoon at a time, beating until stiff peaks form and sugar dissolves. Beat in vanilla.

Spread meringue over hot pie filling, carefully sealing to edge of pastry. Bake as directed in each pie recipe. Yield: meringue for one 9-inch pie.

UNBAKED MERINGUE

½ cup sugar
¼ cup light corn syrup
3 tablespoons water
⅛ teaspoon cream of tartar
Dash of salt
2 egg whites

Combine sugar, syrup, water, cream of tartar, and salt in a medium-size heavy saucepan. Cook over medium heat, stirring frequently, until mixture comes to a boil and sugar dissolves. Remove from heat.

Beat egg whites (at room temperature) in a medium glass or metal mixing bowl until foamy. While beating at medium speed of an electric mixer, slowly pour hot syrup mixture in a thin stream over egg whites. Turn mixer to high speed; beat until stiff peaks form and meringue is thick enough to spread.

Spread meringue immediately over pie filling, carefully sealing to edge of pastry. Yield: meringue for one 10-inch pie.

Cracking an egg with one hand takes finesse; not everyone has it.

PINEAPPLE MERINGUE

3 egg whites
¼ cup plus 2 tablespoons sugar
½ cup crushed pineapple, drained

Beat egg whites (at room temperature) in a medium glass or metal mixing bowl until foamy. Gradually add sugar, 1 tablespoon at a time, beating until stiff peaks form. Fold in pineapple. Spread meringue over hot pie filling, carefully sealing to edge of pastry. Bake as directed in each pie recipe. Yield: meringue for one 9-inch pie.

Meringue: Let's demystify it! Have egg whites at room temperature. The copper bowl-wire whisk routine is not mandatory; cream of tartar sets up a similar stabilizing reaction, so any grease-free bowl and beater will do, except plastic. Look for gloss, sharp peaks, and almost invisible air pockets. Spoon onto hot filling, sealing it to the crust. Cut with a wet knife.

PICK OF THE CROP

Fruit and Berry Pies

Apples were cultivated in the Old World more than 7,000 years before Christ but did not arrive in America until the English brought them. Getting apples planted was a top priority when people settled new territory unless they found apple trees already there, planted by itinerant hunters and trappers. John Chapman earned the title of Johnny Appleseed for his part in the spread of apples cross-country.

Apples, then, could not have been among the first of the sweet pie fillings the colonials enjoyed here; wild berries had to predate them. But apples were ever the longed-for favorite. The wife of a cavalry lieutenant stationed at Fort Lincoln, Dakota Territory, around 1875, recalled paying $25 for a barrel of apples to be shipped from Oregon by oxcart in the fall. To her horror, they arrived frozen.

As has been mentioned, it was once the custom to omit the under crust altogether, using only an edging of puff paste on the rim of the plate. This was the style at Williamsburg. Sometimes an under crust, less rich, was employed, and only the upper crust was made of puff paste. It may be that unruly ovens could not be trusted not to ruin good pastry, or just that, as a practical matter, puff won't puff if it is weighted down. One thing is certain: In the best dining rooms, the cook looked to the beauty of her "upper crust," and the term came to stand for a social stratum.

A custom well worth reviving has to do with leaving the top unsealed from the bottom crust. After baking and cooling, the top crust was lifted off, frothed cream or a cooked sauce poured in, and the top replaced. Nice surprise!

Nowhere in the world do fresh peaches, figs and muscadines, guavas, loquats and mangoes collide with pastry as unforgettably as in the Southern kitchen. Just to the north of the tropical South, enough apples grow to make an endless delight for us all, and throughout the region the wild berries continue to proliferate as they did in the beginning. The urban cook does not usually have a fair chance at the wild goodies, but sometimes a handicap may be overcome by guile: Cultivate a friend in the country!

Back to front: Blueberry Cobbler Roll (page 47) to glaze and serve warm, Plant City Strawberry Pie (page 49) named for a major berry producing area in Florida, and Apple-Cranberry Pie with Cheese Pastry (page 32).

Duncan Hines Apple Pie sits among varieties of cooking apples.

DUNCAN HINES APPLE PIE

Pastry for 1 double-crust
  (9-inch) pie
½ cup sugar
3 tablespoons all-purpose
  flour
¼ teaspoon ground
  nutmeg
¼ cup orange juice
1½ tablespoons light
  corn syrup
2½ tablespoons butter or
  margarine, melted
8 medium-size cooking
  apples, peeled, cored,
  and thinly sliced

Roll half of pastry to ⅛-inch thickness on a lightly floured surface; fit into a 9-inch pie-plate. Set aside.

Combine sugar, flour, nutmeg, orange juice, syrup, and butter in a large mixing bowl; stir well. Add apples, stirring lightly to coat; spoon filling into pastry shell.

Roll remaining pastry to ⅛-inch thickness; place over filling. Trim edges; seal and flute. Cut slits in top crust to allow steam to escape. Bake at 375° for 15 minutes. Reduce heat to 300°, and bake an additional 45 minutes. Cool pie before slicing. Yield: one 9-inch pie.

Hines in his kitchen, 1946.

COUNTRY APPLE PIE

Pastry for 1 double-crust
  (9-inch) pie
6 cups peeled, cored, and
  sliced cooking apples
1 tablespoon lemon juice
½ cup sugar
½ cup firmly packed brown
  sugar
2 tablespoons all-purpose
  flour
½ teaspoon ground cinnamon
¼ teaspoon ground nutmeg
¼ teaspoon salt
2 tablespoons butter or
  margarine

Roll half of pastry to ⅛-inch thickness on a lightly floured surface; fit into a 9-inch pie-plate. Set aside.

Combine apples and lemon juice in a large mixing bowl.

Combine sugar, flour, cinnamon, nutmeg, and salt, mixing well. Spoon over apple mixture, tossing gently. Spoon filling evenly into pastry shell, and dot with butter.

Roll remaining pastry to ⅛-inch thickness, and place over filling. Trim edges; seal and flute. Cut slits in top crust to allow steam to escape. Cover edges of pie with aluminum foil. Bake at 450° for 15 minutes. Reduce heat to 350°, and bake an additional 35 minutes. Yield: one 9-inch pie.

Duncan Hines, a native of Bowling Green, Kentucky, made a name for himself by rating restaurants, writing on food, and putting his name on a line of baking mixes. In his book, *Duncan Hines' Food Odyssey*, he compared Northern and Southern hospitality: Southerners traditionally entertain at home more frequently than Northerners. In his opinion, Southern home cooking was superior to restaurant food.

Old alphabet book uses apple pie to say "A" is for apple.

APPLE-PECAN PIE

¼ cup butter or margarine,
  softened
⅔ cup pecan halves
1 cup firmly packed brown
  sugar, divided
Pastry for 1 double-crust
  (9-inch) pie
5 medium-size cooking
  apples, peeled, cored, and
  thinly sliced
2 tablespoons lemon juice
1 tablespoon all-purpose flour
½ teaspoon ground cinnamon
½ teaspoon ground nutmeg
¼ teaspoon salt
Vanilla ice cream (optional)

Spread butter evenly on bottom and sides of a 9-inch pie-plate. Arrange pecan halves around side and on bottom of pieplate, pressing into butter layer. Sprinkle ⅔ cup sugar over pecan layer in bottom of pieplate, pressing down gently.

Roll half of pastry to ⅛-inch thickness on a lightly floured surface. Place pastry over sugar-pecan layer, leaving a ½-inch overhang around edge of pieplate. Set aside.

Combine apples and lemon juice in a large mixing bowl, and set aside.

Combine flour, cinnamon, nutmeg, salt, and remaining ⅓ cup sugar; mix well. Sprinkle over apples, tossing well. Spoon apple mixture into pastry shell.

Roll remaining pastry to ⅛-inch thickness, and place over filling. Trim edges; seal and flute. Cut slits in top crust to allow steam to escape. Bake at 450° for 10 minutes. Reduce heat to 350°, and bake an additional 40 to 50 minutes. Let pie cool in pieplate for 2 minutes. Invert pie onto a serving plate. Carefully remove pieplate. Serve pie hot with vanilla ice cream, if desired. Yield: one 9-inch pie.

"Pastry making" from lithograph published as a teaching aid by L. Prang & Co., 1875.

PRALINE-TOPPED APPLE PIE

½ cup firmly packed brown sugar
2 tablespoons all-purpose flour
⅓ cup chopped pecans
⅓ cup plus 3 tablespoons light corn syrup, divided
¼ cup plus 1 tablespoon butter or margarine, melted and divided
Pastry for 1 double-crust (9-inch) pie
6 medium-size cooking apples, peeled, cored, and thinly sliced
3 tablespoons sugar
1 tablespoon cornstarch
1 teaspoon ground cinnamon
½ teaspoon salt

Combine brown sugar, flour, and pecans in a small mixing bowl; stir well. Add 3 tablespoons syrup and 3 tablespoons butter, mixing until well blended. Set aside.

Roll half of pastry to ⅛-inch thickness on a lightly floured surface; fit into a 9-inch pie-plate. Top with apple slices, and set aside.

Combine sugar, cornstarch, cinnamon, salt, and remaining syrup and butter; stir well. Pour syrup mixture over apple slices.

Roll remaining pastry to ⅛-inch thickness, and place over filling. Trim edges; seal and flute. Cut slits in top crust to allow steam to escape. Bake at 425° for 25 minutes; remove from oven, and crumble reserved brown sugar mixture over top crust. Reduce heat to 350°, and bake an additional 10 minutes or until topping melts. Cool 10 minutes. Yield: one 9-inch pie.

CRUMB-TOPPED APPLE PIE

½ cup all-purpose flour
⅓ cup sugar
⅓ cup butter or margarine, softened
½ cup sugar
½ cup firmly packed brown sugar
2 tablespoons all-purpose flour
¼ teaspoon ground cinnamon
¼ teaspoon ground nutmeg
¼ teaspoon ground ginger
⅛ teaspoon ground allspice
2 teaspoons grated orange rind
1 tablespoon orange juice
7 medium-size cooking apples, peeled, cored, and thinly sliced
1 unbaked (9-inch) pastry shell
Grated sharp Cheddar cheese (optional)

Combine ½ cup flour and ⅓ cup sugar in a small mixing bowl; cut in butter with a pastry blender until mixture resembles coarse meal. Set aside.

Combine ½ cup sugar, brown sugar, 2 tablespoons flour, spices, orange rind, and juice in a large mixing bowl. Add apples, tossing lightly to coat evenly.

Spoon apple mixture into pastry shell. Sprinkle reserved flour mixture evenly over apples. Bake at 425° for 10 minutes. Reduce heat to 350°, and bake an additional 40 to 50 minutes. Cool before slicing. Serve pie with cheese, if desired. Yield: one 9-inch pie.

TRAVELLERS' REST SKILLET APPLE PIE

1¼ cups sugar
¼ cup all-purpose flour
1 teaspoon ground cinnamon
¼ teaspoon ground nutmeg
⅛ teaspoon salt
3 tablespoons butter or margarine, melted
7 cups peeled, cored, and thinly sliced cooking apples
Pastry (recipe follows)

Combine first 6 ingredients in a large mixing bowl, mixing well. Add apples, and toss gently.

Roll half of pastry to ⅛-inch thickness on a lightly floured surface; fit into a 10-inch cast-iron skillet. Spoon filling evenly into pastry shell.

Roll remaining pastry to ⅛-inch thickness. Cut into ¾-inch-wide strips, and arrange in a lattice fashion over filling. Seal edges to side of skillet. Bake at 400° for 40 minutes or until crust is golden brown. Yield: one 10-inch pie.

Pastry:

2½ cups all-purpose flour
½ teaspoon salt
¼ cup shortening
½ cup cold butter or margarine, cut into small pieces
6 to 8 tablespoons cold water

Combine flour and salt; cut in shortening and butter until mixture resembles coarse meal. Sprinkle water evenly over mixture; stir gently with a fork until mixture forms a ball. Chill 30 minutes. Yield: pastry for one 10-inch double-crust pie.

Skillet Apple Pie photographed at Travellers' Rest.

APPLE-CRANBERRY PIE WITH CHEESE PASTRY

2 cups fresh cranberries
½ cup water
1½ cups sugar
½ cup all-purpose flour
½ teaspoon ground cinnamon
½ teaspoon ground nutmeg
⅛ teaspoon salt
2 tablespoons butter or margarine
3 cups peeled, cored, and thinly sliced cooking apples
Double-Crust Cheese Pastry

Combine cranberries and water in a large saucepan; bring to a boil. Reduce heat; cook 5 minutes or until the cranberries have popped.

Combine sugar, flour, cinnamon, nutmeg, and salt; add to cranberries. Cook over medium heat, stirring constantly, until thickened. Stir in butter and apples. Remove mixture from heat, and cool.

Roll half of pastry to ⅛-inch thickness on a lightly floured surface; fit into a 9-inch pie-plate. Spoon cooled filling into pastry shell.

Roll remaining pastry to ⅛-inch thickness, and place over filling. Trim edges; seal and flute. Cut slits in top crust to allow steam to escape.

Bake at 375° for 55 minutes or until crust is lightly browned. Cool before serving. Yield: one 9-inch pie.

Double-Crust Cheese Pastry:

1½ cups all-purpose flour
½ teaspoon salt
½ cup butter or margarine
¾ cup (3 ounces) shredded sharp Cheddar cheese
3 to 4 tablespoons cold water

Combine flour and salt; cut in butter and cheese with a pastry blender until mixture resembles coarse meal. Sprinkle evenly with water, 1 tablespoon at a time. Stir with a fork until dry ingredients are thoroughly moistened. Shape dough into a ball; chill. Yield: pastry for one 9-inch double-crust pie.

SEPTEMBER.

Apple-tree, apple-tree, crowned with delight,
Give me your fruit for a pie if you will;——
Crusty I'll make it, and juicy and light!——
Give me your treasure to mate with my skill!

Collection of Bonnie Slotnick

Illustration from A Thousand Ways to Please a Husband, *1922.*

APPLE PIE GOODY

1 cup sugar
¾ cup plus 2 tablespoons all-purpose flour, divided
½ teaspoon salt, divided
¼ teaspoon ground nutmeg
¼ teaspoon ground cinnamon
1 (20-ounce) can sliced apples, undrained
½ teaspoon vanilla extract
¾ cup quick-cooking oats, uncooked
¾ cup firmly packed brown sugar
¼ teaspoon baking powder
¼ teaspoon baking soda
½ cup butter or margarine, melted
Vanilla ice cream

Combine sugar, 2 tablespoons flour, ¼ teaspoon salt, nutmeg, and cinnamon in a mixing bowl; stir well. Add apples and vanilla, stirring until well combined. Pour apple mixture into a greased 10- x 6- x 2-inch baking dish; set aside.

Combine remaining flour and salt, oats, brown sugar, baking powder, and soda; stir well. Add butter, and stir until well blended. Crumble oat mixture over apple mixture. Bake at 350° for 40 minutes or until golden brown and bubbly. Serve warm with vanilla ice cream. Yield: 10 servings.

KENTUCKY APPLE COBBLER

7 cups peeled, cored, and sliced cooking apples
1 tablespoon lemon juice
¾ cup sugar
¼ cup all-purpose flour
½ teaspoon grated lemon rind
¼ teaspoon ground nutmeg
¼ teaspoon ground cinnamon
⅛ teaspoon salt
2 tablespoons butter or margarine
Pastry for one (9-inch) pie

Combine apples and lemon juice in a large mixing bowl. Combine sugar, flour, lemon rind, nutmeg, cinnamon, and salt. Spoon over apple mixture; toss lightly to coat well.

Spoon filling evenly into a greased 9-inch pieplate, and dot with butter.

Roll pastry to ⅛-inch thickness on a lightly-floured surface; place over apple mixture. Trim edges; seal and flute. Cut slits in top crust to allow steam to escape. Bake at 350° for 1 hour. Cool 10 minutes before serving. Yield: about 8 servings.

APPLE POT PIE

2 cups all-purpose flour
¼ teaspoon salt
⅓ cup butter or margarine
½ cup cold water
1½ cups sugar
1½ teaspoons ground cinnamon
7 medium-size cooking apples, peeled, cored, and chopped
¼ cup butter or margarine
2 cups water
Vanilla ice cream

Combine flour and salt in a medium mixing bowl; cut in ⅓ cup butter with a pastry blender until mixture resembles coarse meal. Sprinkle ½ cup cold water evenly over surface; stir with a fork until dry ingredients are moistened. Shape dough into a ball; chill.

Combine sugar and cinnamon; set aside.

Roll dough into an 18- x 12-inch rectangle on a lightly floured surface; cut dough into 2-inch squares.

Layer apples, sugar mixture, ¼ cup butter, and dough in a 3-quart saucepan. Add 2 cups water to saucepan. Cover and simmer 20 minutes; uncover and simmer 15 minutes or until thickened. Spoon hot pie into individual serving dishes, and serve with vanilla ice cream. Yield: 8 to 10 servings.

Apple Gathering, *oil on canvas, by Jerome B. Thompson, 1814-1886.*

Parson Weems' Fable *by Grant Wood. Oil on canvas, 1939.*

MOUNT VERNON RED CHERRY PIE

2 (16-ounce) cans tart
  cherries, drained
1 cup sugar
2½ tablespoons cornstarch
⅛ teaspoon salt
Pastry for 1 double-crust
  (9-inch) pie

Combine cherries, sugar, cornstarch, and salt in a medium saucepan; stir until well blended. Set aside for 10 minutes. Cook over medium heat 15 minutes or until thickened, stirring occasionally. Cool slightly.

Roll half of pastry to ⅛-inch thickness on a lightly floured surface; fit into a 9-inch pieplate. Spoon cherry mixture into pastry shell.

Roll remaining pastry to ⅛-inch thickness; cut into ¾-inch-wide strips, and arrange in a lattice fashion over filling. Trim edges; seal and flute. Bake at 450° for 15 minutes. Reduce heat to 400°; bake an additional 20 minutes. (Cover edges of pie with aluminum foil to prevent overbrowning, if necessary.) Cool before slicing. Yield: one 9-inch pie.

Folklore has to come from somewhere, and in the case of the story about George Washington cutting down the cherry tree, we know it was a fabrication of Anglican clergyman, Mason Locke Weems. In his biography of Washington, his wish was to enrich our heritage by fleshing out and humanizing Washington the man. Artist Grant Wood, also a romanticist, satirized the story by painting Weems pulling back the curtain on the fable he had created.

Cherry Desserts

ROYAL ANNE CHERRY PIE

1 (16-ounce) can Royal Anne
  cherries, undrained
½ cup sugar
2 tablespoons cornstarch
¼ teaspoon salt
2 tablespoons butter or
  margarine
2 tablespoons lemon juice
½ cup chopped walnuts
1 baked (9-inch) pastry shell
3 egg whites
¼ cup plus 2 tablespoons
  sugar
½ teaspoon almond extract

Drain cherries, reserving liquid. Set aside.

Combine ½ cup sugar, cornstarch, and salt in a heavy saucepan. Gradually stir in the reserved liquid. Cook over medium heat 10 minutes or until thickened and bubbly, stirring constantly. Remove from heat. Add butter; stir until butter melts. Stir in cherries, lemon juice, and walnuts. Pour filling into pastry shell.

Beat egg whites (at room temperature) until foamy. Gradually add ¼ cup plus 2 tablespoons sugar, 1 tablespoon at a time, beating until stiff peaks form. Beat in almond extract. Spread meringue over filling, sealing to edge of pastry. Bake at 350° for 10 minutes or until meringue is lightly browned. Cool to room temperature. Chill. Yield: one 9-inch pie.

FIG PIE

3 cups fresh or canned figs,
  quartered and drained
1 unbaked (9-inch) pastry
  shell
2 eggs, beaten
¼ cup plus 2 tablespoons
  sugar
2 tablespoons all-purpose
  flour
2 tablespoons butter or
  margarine, melted
2 tablespoons lemon juice
2 teaspoons ground ginger
Whipped cream

Place figs in pastry shell. Combine eggs, sugar, flour, butter, lemon juice, and ginger in a medium mixing bowl; beat well. Pour over figs in pastry shell.

Bake at 450° for 10 minutes. Reduce heat to 350°, and continue baking 30 minutes. Cool. Serve with whipped cream. Yield: one 9-inch pie.

FIG STREUSEL PIE

½ cup all-purpose flour
½ cup firmly packed brown
  sugar
½ cup butter or margarine
1 unbaked (9-inch) pastry
  shell
3 cups fresh figs, quartered
½ cup sugar
½ teaspoon ground cinnamon
1 egg, beaten
2 tablespoons evaporated
  milk
¼ teaspoon almond extract

Combine flour and brown sugar in a medium mixing bowl; cut in butter using a pastry blender. Spoon half of mixture into pastry shell. Set remaining mixture aside. Arrange figs evenly over butter mixture.

Combine sugar and cinnamon; sprinkle evenly over figs. Combine egg, milk, and almond extract; beat well, and pour over figs. Top with remaining butter mixture.

Bake at 400° for 40 minutes. (Cover edges of pie with aluminum foil to prevent overbrowning, if necessary). Cool slightly. Yield: one 9-inch pie.

Mount Vernon Red Cherry Pie: Lattice topping in progress.

FRESH FIG COBBLER

Pastry for 1 double-crust
(10-inch) deep-dish pie
¾ cup firmly packed brown
sugar
½ cup sugar
⅓ cup all-purpose flour
1 teaspoon grated orange rind
⅛ teaspoon ground ginger
4 cups sliced fresh figs
1½ tablespoons butter or
margarine

Roll half of pastry to ⅛-inch
thickness on a lightly floured
surface; fit into a 10-inch deep-
dish pieplate. Set aside.

Combine sugar, flour, orange
rind, and ginger in a large mixing bowl; stir well. Add figs; toss
lightly to coat well. Spoon mixture into pastry shell; dot with
butter.

Roll remaining pastry to ⅛-
inch thickness; cut into ¾-inch-
wide strips, and arrange in a lattice fashion over figs. Trim
edges; seal and flute. Bake at
400° for 10 minutes. Reduce
heat to 375°, and bake an additional 40 minutes. Yield: 8 to 10
servings.

MUSCADINE PIE

Pastry for 1 double-crust
(9-inch) pie
3½ pounds ripe muscadines
1 tablespoon fresh lemon
juice
¼ cup all-purpose flour
1 to 1½ cups sugar
2 tablespoons butter or
margarine

Roll half of pastry to ⅛-inch
thickness on a lightly floured
surface; fit into a 9-inch pieplate. Set aside.

Wash and mash muscadines.
Separate hulls from pulp; set
hulls aside. Strain pulp, reserving juice; discard pulp and
seeds. Combine juice and hulls
in a heavy saucepan; cover and
cook over low heat 20 minutes
or until hulls are tender. Cool.

Combine hull mixture, lemon
juice, flour, and sugar; mix well.
Pour into prepared pastry shell;
dot with butter.

Roll remaining pastry to ⅛-
inch thickness; cut into ¾-inch-
wide strips, and arrange in a lattice fashion over filling. Trim
edges; seal and flute. Bake at
400° for 10 minutes. Reduce
heat to 375°, and bake 25 to 30
additional minutes. Yield: one
9-inch pie.

The muscadine grape-
vine grows tall in the
South, bearing small
clusters of thick-skinned,
musky fruit. It is one of the
sources of several cultivated
grapes, including the scup-
pernong, another grape pe-
culiar to Southern climes.

Polish farm buyers examine grape vines in North Carolina, 1914.

GREEN GRAPE COBBLER

Pastry (recipe follows)
6 cups seedless green grapes,
  washed and cut in half
¾ cup sugar
3 tablespoons cornstarch
1½ tablespoons lemon juice
1 tablespoon butter or
  margarine, softened

Roll half of pastry to ⅛-inch thickness on a lightly floured surface; fit pastry into a 1-quart casserole. Set remaining pastry aside.

Combine grapes and water to cover in a medium saucepan; cover and cook over medium heat 10 minutes or until grapes are soft. Drain off liquid, reserving grapes in saucepan. Add sugar, cornstarch, and lemon juice to saucepan, stirring well. Cook over medium heat, stirring occasionally, until thickened. Stir in butter; pour mixture into pastry shell.

Roll remaining pastry to ⅛-inch thickness; place over filling. Trim edges; seal and flute. Cut slits in top crust to allow steam to escape. Bake at 350° for 30 minutes or until lightly browned. Yield: 6 servings.

Pastry:

2½ cups all-purpose flour
½ cup sugar
1 egg, beaten
1 teaspoon baking powder
¼ teaspoon salt
2 tablespoons butter or
  margarine, melted
2 tablespoons milk

Combine all ingredients, mixing well to form a smooth ball. Chill. Yield: pastry for a 1-quart cobbler.

Lemon Slice Pie: Glazed top crust is crisp and spicy.

LEMON SLICE PIE

Pastry for 1 double-crust
  (9-inch) pie
1 medium lemon
1¼ cups plus 2 teaspoons
  sugar, divided
2 tablespoons all-purpose
  flour
⅛ teaspoon salt
¼ cup butter or margarine,
  melted
3 eggs, beaten
1½ tablespoons lemon
  juice
1 egg white, slightly beaten
⅛ teaspoon ground
  cinnamon

Roll half of pastry to ⅛-inch thickness on a lightly floured surface; fit into a 9-inch pie-plate. Set aside.

Grate rind from lemon; set rind aside. Cut lemon into thin slices; remove and discard seeds and any remaining rind from slices. Set lemon slices aside.

Combine 1¼ cups sugar, flour, and salt in a large mixing bowl; add butter, eggs, and lemon juice, stirring well. Add reserved grated lemon rind and slices, stirring well. Pour lemon mixture into pastry shell.

Roll remaining pastry to ⅛-inch thickness, and place over filling. Trim edges of pastry; seal and flute. Cut slits in top crust to allow steam to ecape. Brush pastry lightly with beaten egg white; sprinkle with remaining 2 teaspoons sugar and cinnamon. Bake at 400° for 15 minutes. Reduce heat to 375°, and bake an additional 15 minutes. Let cool before slicing. Yield: one 9-inch pie.

MANGO PIE

LOQUAT COBBLER

Pastry for 1 double-crust
(9-inch) pie
1 cup sugar
2 tablespoons all-purpose
flour
½ teaspoon ground
cinnamon
¼ teaspoon ground nutmeg
3½ cups peeled, sliced
mangoes
1 tablespoon lemon juice
1 tablespoon butter or
margarine

Roll half of pastry to ⅛-inch
thickness on a lightly floured
surface; fit into a 9-inch pieplate. Set aside.

Combine sugar, flour, cinnamon, and nutmeg in a small
mixing bowl. Set aside.

Arrange half of mangoes in
pastry shell; sprinkle with half
of sugar mixture. Repeat layers.
Sprinkle with lemon juice; dot
with butter.

Roll remaining pastry to ⅛-
inch thickness; place over filling. Trim edges; seal and flute.
Cut slits in top crust to allow
steam to escape. Bake at 425°
for 10 minutes on lowest oven
rack. Reduce heat to 350°; bake
an additional 35 minutes. Cool.
Yield: one 9-inch pie.

*Florida fruit
exhibit,
1844-1845.*

1 cup sugar
2 tablespoons all-purpose
flour
2 (15-ounce) cans pitted
loquats, drained
1 tablespoon lemon juice
1 tablespoon butter or
margarine
Pastry for 1 (10-inch) pie

Combine sugar and flour in a
medium mixing bowl; stir well.
Add loquats, and toss gently to
coat. Place loquat mixture in a
greased 10- x 6- x 2-inch baking
dish; sprinkle with lemon juice.
Dot with butter.

Roll pastry to ⅛-inch thickness on a lightly floured surface.
Place over loquat mixture, leaving a ½-inch overhang around
edge of dish. Turn pastry edges
under; press firmly to rim of
baking dish to seal, and flute.
Cut slits in crust to allow steam
to escape. Bake at 400° for 40
minutes or until lightly
browned. Yield: 6 to 8 servings.

The mango is probably
native to India, but it
has been making itself
at home in the deep South
for many years. In size, color,
and shape, it varies widely,
weighing anywhere from a
few ounces to five pounds. It
may be green to yellow to red.
Long ago, street vendors in
Florida sold mangoes from
trucks, crying "Mango! Ripe
Mango!" as they cruised the
neighborhoods. Underripe
mangoes are valued as the
base for chutney, while the
semiripe to ripe ones go into
pies and salads. Mangoes are
also delightful when simply
halved and served with a
spoon. It is difficult for
mango lovers in the upper
South to get perfect man-
goes; they can be heavy-
seeded and fibrous.

Peach Season, painted in Dyer, Arkansas, by Fannie Lou Spelce.

FRESH PEACH MERINGUE PIE

½ cup butter or margarine, softened
1 cup sugar
6 egg yolks
2 tablespoons all-purpose flour
2½ cups peeled, sliced fresh peaches
1 unbaked (9-inch) pastry shell
4 egg whites
½ cup sugar

Cream butter in a mixing bowl. Gradually add 1 cup sugar; beat well. Add yolks and flour; mix well. Fold in peaches. Pour mixture into pastry shell. Bake at 350° for 40 minutes.

Beat egg whites (at room temperature) until foamy. Add ½ cup sugar, 1 tablespoon at a time, beating until stiff peaks form. Spread meringue over filling; seal to edge of pastry. Bake at 350° for 8 minutes or until golden brown. Cool and refrigerate. Yield: one 9-inch pie.

GEORGIA PEACH PIE

Pastry for 1 double-crust (9-inch) pie
½ cup sugar
½ cup firmly packed brown sugar
3 tablespoons quick-cooking tapioca
⅛ teaspoon salt
5 cups peeled, sliced fresh peaches
⅛ teaspoon almond extract
1 tablespoon butter or margarine

Roll half of pastry to ⅛-inch thickness on a lightly floured surface; fit into a 9-inch pie-plate. Set aside.

Combine sugar, tapioca, and salt in a large mixing bowl. Add peaches, and toss gently to coat. Stir in almond extract. Pour peach mixture into pastry shell; dot with butter.

Roll remaining pastry to ⅛-inch thickness, and place over filling. Trim edges; seal and flute. Cut slits in top crust to allow steam to escape. Bake at 450° for 10 minutes. Reduce heat to 375°, and bake an additional 40 minutes or until crust is golden brown. Yield: one 9-inch pie.

GLAZED PEACH PIE

1 cup sugar
2 tablespoons cornstarch
½ cup water
3 pounds fresh, ripe peaches
¼ teaspoon almond extract
1 baked (9-inch) pastry shell

Combine sugar, cornstarch, and water in a heavy saucepan; stir well.

Peel and slice 6 peaches; add peaches to sugar mixture. Cook over medium heat, stirring constantly, until mixture is thickened and bubbly. Cool. Stir in almond extract.

Peel and slice remaining peaches. Arrange peach slices in pastry shell. Pour glaze over peaches, coating well. Chill. Yield: one 9-inch pie.

EASY PEACH COBBLER

4 cups frozen sliced peaches, thawed
½ cup sugar
½ cup butter or margarine
1 cup all-purpose flour
1 cup sugar
1½ teaspoons baking powder
½ teaspoon salt
¾ cup milk
Vanilla ice cream

Combine peaches and ½ cup sugar; let stand 10 minutes.

Melt butter in a 12- x 8- x 2-inch baking dish; set aside.

Combine flour, 1 cup sugar, baking powder, and salt in a medium mixing bowl; add milk, mixing well. Pour batter into prepared baking dish (do not stir). Pour peach mixture evenly over batter.

Bake at 375° for 50 minutes or until golden brown. Serve warm with ice cream. Yield: 6 to 8 servings.

PEACH COBBLER SUPREME

2 cups plus 1 tablespoon sugar, divided
¼ cup all-purpose flour
½ teaspoon ground nutmeg
10 cups peeled, sliced fresh peaches
1 teaspoon almond extract
⅓ cup butter or margarine, melted
Pastry (recipe follows)

Combine 2 cups sugar, flour, and nutmeg in a large Dutch oven; add peaches, and set aside 15 minutes. Bring peach mixture to a boil. Reduce heat; cook over low heat, stirring occasionally, 10 minutes or until peaches are tender and mixture thickens. Remove from heat; add almond extract and butter. Stir gently until butter melts. Set aside.

Roll one-third of pastry to ⅛-inch thickness on a lightly floured surface; cut into ¾-inch-wide strips, and place on an ungreased baking sheet. Bake at 425° for 10 to 12 minutes or until golden brown. Cool completely, and set aside.

Roll half of remaining pastry to ⅛-inch thickness; fit into a 12- x 8- x 2-inch baking dish.

Spoon half of peach mixture into pastry shell; arrange cooked pastry strips evenly over filling. Spoon remaining peach mixture over pastry strips.

Roll remaining pastry to ⅛-inch thickness; cut into ¾-inch-wide strips, and arrange in a lattice fashion over filling. Trim edges; seal and flute. Sprinkle remaining sugar on lattice strips.

Bake at 475° for 15 minutes. Reduce temperature to 375°, and bake an additional 20 minutes. Yield: 8 servings.

Pastry:

4½ cups all-purpose flour
1 teaspoon salt
1½ cups shortening
1 cup plus 2 tablespoons water

Combine flour and salt in a mixing bowl; cut in shortening with a pastry blender until mixture resembles coarse meal. Sprinkle water evenly over flour mixture, 1 tablespoon at a time, and stir with a fork until all ingredients are moistened. Shape dough into a ball; chill. Yield: pastry for a 12- x 8- x 2-inch baking dish.

Perfect peaches and berries on fruit vinegar label, c.1900.

PEAR CRUMBLE PIE

7 medium pears, peeled,
  cored, and cut into
  ½-inch-thick slices
  (about 5 cups)
¾ cup sugar
1 teaspoon grated lemon rind
3 tablespoons lemon juice
1 unbaked (9-inch) pastry
  shell
½ cup all-purpose flour
½ cup sugar
1 teaspoon ground nutmeg
½ teaspoon ground cinnamon
¼ teaspoon ground mace
⅓ cup butter or margarine

Combine pears, ¾ cup sugar,
lemon rind, and juice in a large
mixing bowl; toss well. Spoon
pear mixture into pastry shell.

Combine flour, ½ cup sugar,
nutmeg, cinnamon, and mace
in a small bowl; cut in butter
with a pastry blender until mixture resembles coarse meal.
Sprinkle mixture evenly over
pears. Bake at 350° for 1 hour.
Cool. Yield: one 9-inch pie.

PEAR MINCEMEAT PIE

6½ pounds pears, peeled,
  cored, and cubed
Grated rind of 1 large orange
Grated rind of 1 large lemon
Juice of 1 large orange
Juice of 1 large lemon
1 large cooking apple, peeled,
  cored, and cubed
6 cups sugar
1 (15-ounce) package raisins
1 cup grape juice
⅔ cup vinegar
2 teaspoons ground cloves
2 teaspoons ground mace
1 teaspoon salt
3 unbaked (9-inch) pastry
  shells

Combine all ingredients, except pastry shells, in a non-aluminum stock pot; bring to a
boil. Cook, uncovered, over low
heat 2 hours or until thickened,
stirring occasionally.

Pour 4 cups filling into each
pastry shell. Bake at 425° for 40
minutes. Cool before slicing.
Yield: three 9-inch pies.

Old-Fashioned Pear Pie with variation on lattice topping.

OLD-FASHIONED PEAR PIE

Pastry for 1 double-crust
  (9-inch) pie
1 cup sugar, divided
3 tablespoons cornstarch
1 teaspoon ground cinnamon
¼ teaspoon ground nutmeg
⅛ teaspoon salt
9 cups peeled, cored, and
  sliced pears
¼ cup all-purpose flour
3 tablespoons butter or
  margarine, melted
2 tablespoons brandy
1 tablespoon lemon juice
1 egg white, beaten

Roll half of pastry to ⅛-inch
thickness on a lightly floured
surface; fit into a 9-inch pieplate. Set aside.

Combine ½ cup sugar, cornstarch, cinnamon, nutmeg, and
salt in a large mixing bowl. Add
pears, tossing gently to coat.
Spoon into pastry shell.

Combine remaining sugar,
flour, butter, brandy, and lemon
juice; mix well. Spoon over pear
mixture.

Roll remaining pastry to ⅛-
inch thickness; cut into ½-inch-
wide strips, and arrange in a lattice fashion over filling. Trim
edges; seal and flute. Bake at
350° for 55 minutes. Brush
pastry with egg white, and continue baking 5 minutes or until
pastry is golden brown. Yield:
one 9-inch pie.

PERSIMMON PIE

1 cup persimmon pulp
1½ cups sugar
1 egg, slightly beaten
2 egg yolks, slightly beaten
1 (13-ounce) can evaporated
   milk
1 tablespoon cornstarch
¼ teaspoon ground nutmeg
½ teaspoon salt
1 unbaked (9-inch) pastry
   shell
Whipped cream

Combine persimmon pulp and sugar in a medium mixing bowl; beat well. Add egg, egg yolks, milk, cornstarch, nutmeg, and salt; beat until well blended.

Pour persimmon mixture into pastry shell. Bake at 350° for 1 hour or until a knife inserted in center comes out clean. Cool. Garnish with dollops of whipped cream. Yield: one 9-inch pie.

PLUM MERINGUE PIE

1½ cups sugar
⅓ cup all-purpose flour
2 eggs, separated
1½ cups puréed plum pulp
½ cup water
1 baked (9-inch) pastry shell
¼ teaspoon cream of tartar
¼ cup sugar

Combine 1½ cups sugar, flour, egg yolks, plum pulp, and water in a medium-size non-aluminum saucepan. Cook over medium heat, stirring constantly, until thickened and bubbly. Pour into pastry shell.

Beat egg whites (at room temperature) and cream of tartar until foamy. Gradually add ¼ cup sugar, 1 tablespoon at a time, beating until stiff peaks form. Spread meringue over filling, sealing to edge of pastry. Bake at 350° for 12 minutes or until meringue is golden brown. Yield: one 9-inch pie.

I t is thought that rhubarb came from northern Asia via Italy. The earliest reference to it in America is dated in the late 1700s. At first, rhubarb was used only medicinally, not eaten because of its exceedingly acidic flavor; then it was discovered that, sugared heavily, it was delectable. Some home-grown rhubarb is green in color; the flavor is the same as the roseate strains, but it is unattractive when cooked. Look for fresh, crisp, brightly colored pink stalks with no hint of pithiness. However, remember to discard the leaves as they contain enough oxalic acid to be toxic.

Rhubarb on shipping label from Washington Berry Growers Association.

RHUBARB PIE

Lattice-Top Pastry
1½ cups plus 2 tablespoons
    sugar, divided
2 tablespoons cornstarch
½ teaspoon ground
    nutmeg
½ cup orange juice
6 cups sliced rhubarb
2 tablespoons butter or
    margarine
1 egg white, beaten

    Roll half of pastry to ⅛-inch thickness on a lightly floured surface; fit pastry into a 9-inch pieplate, leaving overhang. Set aside.

    Combine 1½ cups sugar, cornstarch, and nutmeg in a medium saucepan; stir mixture to remove lumps. Stir orange juice into sugar mixture. Cook over medium heat, stirring constantly, until mixture thickens. Remove from heat. Add rhubarb and butter, stirring until butter melts. Spoon rhubarb mixture into prepared pastry shell.

    Roll remaining pastry to ⅛-inch thickness, and cut into fourteen 10- x ½-inch strips. Arrange strips in a lattice fashion over filling; press ends gently to seal strips to pastry overhang. Trim and flute. Brush with egg white, and sprinkle with remaining sugar.

    Bake at 450° for 10 minutes. Reduce heat to 350°, and bake an additional 30 minutes or until crust is lightly browned. Cool before serving. Yield: one 9-inch pie.

Lattice-Top Pastry:

2 cups all-purpose flour
½ teaspoon salt
⅔ cup plus 2 tablespoons
    shortening
5 to 6 tablespoons cold
    water

    Combine flour and salt; cut in shortening with a pastry blender until mixture resembles coarse meal. Sprinkle cold water evenly over surface; stir with a fork until all ingredients are moistened. Shape dough into a ball; chill. Yield: pastry for one 9-inch lattice-top pie.

Rhubarb-Strawberry Cobbler, an exceptional combination.

RHUBARB-STRAWBERRY COBBLER

2½ cups sugar
¾ cup all-purpose flour
1 teaspoon salt
6 cups sliced rhubarb
2 cups fresh strawberry
    halves
1 tablespoon lemon juice
¼ cup butter or margarine
Pastry (recipe follows)

    Combine sugar, flour, and salt; mix well. Set aside.

    Combine rhubarb and strawberries; toss lightly to mix.

    Place half of fruit mixture in the bottom of a greased 2½-quart baking dish. Sprinkle half of flour mixture over fruit; repeat procedure with remaining fruit and flour mixture. Sprinkle lemon juice evenly over top, and dot with butter.

    Roll pastry to ¼-inch thickness on a lightly floured surface. Place pastry over fruit mixture, sealing edges to sides of dish. Flute edges of pastry. Cut slits in top crust to allow steam to escape. Bake at 450° for 15 minutes. Reduce heat to 375°, and bake an additional 30 minutes or until crust is golden brown. Yield: 8 to 10 servings.

Pastry:

1½ cups all-purpose flour
½ teaspoon salt
½ cup shortening
¼ cup plus 2 tablespoons
    half-and-half

    Combine flour and salt in a bowl; cut in shortening with a pastry blender until mixture resembles coarse meal. Sprinkle half-and-half evenly over surface; stir with a fork until dry ingredients are moistened. Shape dough into a ball; chill. Yield: pastry for one 2½-quart cobbler.

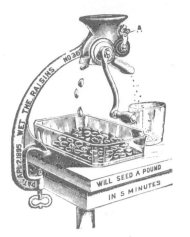

RAISIN PIE

Pastry for 1 double-crust
  (9-inch) pie
1½ cups sugar
1 cup raisins
¼ cup all-purpose flour
¼ teaspoon salt
2 cups water
1 egg, beaten
2 tablespoons grated lemon
  rind
3 tablespoons lemon juice

Roll half of pastry to ⅛-inch thickness on a lightly floured surface; fit into a 9-inch pie-plate. Set aside.

Combine sugar, raisins, flour, salt, and water in a medium saucepan; stir well. Bring to a boil; cook 1 minute, stirring constantly. Remove from heat, and cool 5 minutes.

Gradually stir about one-fourth hot mixture into egg; add to remaining hot mixture, stirring constantly. Pour raisin mixture into top of a double-boiler; place over boiling water, and cook 5 minutes, stirring frequently. Remove from heat, and stir in lemon rind and juice. Cool completely. Pour cooled raisin mixture into pastry shell.

Roll remaining pastry to ⅛-inch thickness; cut into ¾-inch-wide strips, and arrange in a lattice fashion over filling. Trim edges; seal and flute. Bake at 450° for 10 minutes. Reduce heat to 350°, and bake an additional 20 minutes. Yield: one 9-inch pie.

MRS. FITZHUGH LEE'S MINCEMEAT

2 pounds ground chuck,
  cooked and drained
4½ cups diced suet
2¼ cups sugar
2 (15-ounce) packages raisins
1 (10-ounce) package currants
1 cup peeled, diced citron
⅔ cup diced candied lemon
  peel
⅓ cup peeled, diced apple
1 tablespoon grated orange
  rind
2 teaspoons grated lemon
  rind
2 teaspoons freshly grated
  nutmeg
½ teaspoon salt
2 cups Madeira
2 cups brandy
½ cup orange juice
¼ cup lemon juice

Combine all ingredients in a non-aluminum stock pot; stir well. Cover; refrigerate 2 days.

Bring mixture to a boil; reduce heat, and simmer 2 hours, stirring occasionally. Spoon mixture into hot, sterilized jars, leaving ⅛-inch headspace. Adjust lids; process 20 minutes in a boiling-water bath. Yield: 3 quarts.

Prepared mincemeat
"makes an everyday
convenience of an
old-time luxury."
Trade card, c.1900.

MINCEMEAT PIE WITH BOURBON SAUCE

Pastry for 1 double-crust
  (9-inch) pie
4 cups prepared mincemeat
Bourbon Sauce

Roll half of pastry to ⅛-inch thickness on a lightly floured surface; fit into a 9-inch pie-plate. Set aside.

Place mincemeat in a medium saucepan; cook over low heat, stirring occasionally, until thoroughly heated. Spoon mixture into pastry shell.

Roll remaining pastry to ⅛-inch thickness; and place over filling. Trim edges; seal and flute. Cut slits in top crust to allow steam to escape. Bake at 400° for 10 minutes. Reduce heat to 350°, and continue baking 30 minutes. Serve slices with Bourbon Sauce. Yield: one 9-inch pie.

Bourbon Sauce:

½ cup butter or margarine,
  melted
½ cup sugar
½ cup bourbon

Combine butter and sugar in a heavy saucepan; bring mixture to a boil, stirring constantly. Reduce heat; cook 5 minutes or until sugar completely dissolves. Stir in bourbon. Serve immediately over pie slices. Yield: 1 cup.

THE PIE.

See the Pie.

It is a Mince Pie.

It was Sent in by a Kind-Hearted Neighbor.

Well, the Neighbor may have a Right Kind Heart, but She has not got the Right Kind of Shortening for her Pie Crust.

Why Do you say that?

Because this Pie Crust is made with Butter and Lard, and it is Tough and Indigestible. Indeed, to cut this Pie would give one violent exercise.

Let us, then, make a Pie for Ourselves.

We will do so, and for Shortening we will use Cottolene.

What, then, shall we do with the kind neighbor's Pie?

We will throw it away.

"Never Put a Gift Pie in your Mouth."

BERRY PIES

BERRY PIE

1 cup sugar
1 tablespoon plus 1½ teaspoons cornstarch
¼ teaspoon salt
6 cups fresh blackberries, blueberries, or raspberries
2 tablespoons butter or margarine
Pastry for 1 double-crust (9-inch) pie

Combine sugar, cornstarch, and salt in a medium saucepan, stirring well to remove lumps. Add berries; mix well. Cook over low heat, stirring constantly, until mixture is thickened and bubbly. Add butter, mixing well. Set mixture aside, and let cool.

Roll half of pastry to ⅛-inch thickness on a lightly floured surface; fit into a 9-inch pie-plate. Pour cooled berry mixture into pastry shell.

Roll remaining pastry to ⅛-inch thickness; cut into ¾-inch-wide strips, and arrange in a lattice design over filling. Trim edges; seal and flute. Bake at 400° for 20 minutes. Reduce heat to 350°, and continue baking for 30 minutes or until crust is golden brown. Yield: one 9-inch pie.

BERRY COBBLER

1 cup sugar, divided
3 tablespoons butter or margarine, divided
1 cup all-purpose flour
1 teaspoon baking powder
½ teaspoon salt
½ cup milk
1 quart fresh blackberries, blueberries, or raspberries
1 cup boiling water

Combine ½ cup sugar and 1 tablespoon butter in a medium mixing bowl; beat well.

Combine flour, baking powder, and salt; mix well. Add flour mixture to sugar mixture, and mix well. Stir in milk until dry ingredients are moistened. Spread mixture evenly in bottom of a greased 10- x 6- x 2-inch baking dish. Cover dough with berries; sprinkle with remaining sugar. Dot with remaining butter. Pour boiling water over berries. Bake at 350° for 1 hour. Yield: 6 servings.

Note: If substituting frozen berries for fresh, thaw and drain berries, reserving juice. Combine juice and water to yield 1 cup; bring mixture to a boil. Substitute mixture for 1 cup boiling water.

HUCKLEBERRY PIE

Pastry for 1 double-crust (9-inch) pie
4 cups fresh huckleberries or blueberries
¾ cup sugar
1 tablespoon all-purpose flour
1 teaspoon grated lemon rind
2 tablespoons lemon juice
2 tablespoons butter or margarine
Whipping cream
2 teaspoons sugar

Roll half of pastry to ⅛-inch thickness on a lightly floured surface; fit into a 9-inch pie-plate. Chill remaining pastry.

Place huckleberries in pastry shell. Combine ¾ cup sugar and flour; spoon mixture evenly over berries. Sprinkle with lemon rind and juice. Dot with butter.

Roll remaining pastry to ⅛-inch thickness, and place over filling. Trim edges; seal and flute. Cut slits in top pastry to allow steam to escape. Brush top crust (not fluted edge) with whipping cream; sprinkle with 2 teaspoons sugar.

Bake at 425° for 15 minutes. Reduce heat to 350°; continue baking 20 to 25 minutes. (Cover edges with aluminum foil to prevent overbrowning, if necessary.) Yield: one 9-inch pie.

BLUEBERRY COBBLER ROLL

2 cups plus 1½ tablespoons all-purpose flour, divided
½ teaspoon salt
⅔ cup shortening
½ cup half-and-half
½ cup sugar
Dash of salt
1 tablespoon butter or margarine, melted
¼ teaspoon grated lemon rind
2 teaspoons lemon juice
2 cups fresh blueberries
1 cup sifted powdered sugar
2 tablespoons water

Combine 2 cups flour and ½ teaspoon salt in medium mixing bowl; cut in shortening with a pastry blender until mixture resembles coarse meal. Sprinkle half-and-half evenly over mixture; stir with a fork until all ingredients are moistened. Shape dough into a ball; chill.

Combine sugar, dash of salt, and remaining flour; add butter, lemon rind, and juice, stirring well. Fold in blueberries.

Roll pastry into a 12- x 8-inch rectangle on a lightly floured surface. Spread with blueberry mixture. Roll up jellyroll fashion, beginning at long side; moisten edges and ends with water to seal. Transfer roll to a heavily greased 15- x 10- x 1-inch jellyroll pan. Bake at 425° for 40 minutes. Cool 5 minutes. Transfer roll to a serving platter.

Combine powdered sugar and water in a small bowl, mixing well. Drizzle glaze over warm roll. Slice and serve immediately. Yield: 6 to 8 servings.

ackberry is one way to go with Berry Pie recipe.

DEEP-DISH BLACKBERRY COBBLER

Pastry (recipe follows)
4 cups fresh blackberries or 2 (16-ounce) packages frozen blackberries, thawed
1 cup sugar, divided
2 tablespoons all-purpose flour, divided
2 tablespoons butter or margarine, divided
Vanilla ice cream (optional)

Divide pastry into thirds. Roll one portion into an 8-inch square on a lightly floured surface; place on a baking sheet. Bake at 450° for 10 minutes or until lightly browned. Cool.

Roll another portion of pastry to ⅛-inch thickness on a lightly floured surface; fit into an 8-inch square baking dish.

Place half of blackberries in prepared baking dish. Top with ½ cup sugar and 1 tablespoon flour; dot with 1 tablespoon butter. Cover with baked pastry square, remaining blackberries, sugar, flour, and butter.

Roll remaining pastry to ⅛-inch thickness; cut into fourteen 10- x ½-inch strips. Arrange strips in a lattice design over blackberries. Press ends gently to seal strips to pastry overhang; trim edges and flute. Bake at 450° for 10 minutes. Reduce heat to 350°; bake 45 minutes or until golden brown. Serve warm with ice cream, if desired. Yield: 8 servings.

Cranberry Pie: Always a favorite at Christmas.

Pastry:

3 cups all-purpose flour
1½ teaspoons salt
1 cup plus 3 tablespoons shortening
9 to 10 tablespoons water

Combine flour and salt; cut in shortening with a pastry blender until mixture resembles coarse meal. Sprinkle water, 1 tablespoon at a time, over surface; stir with a fork until all ingredients are moistened. Shape dough into a ball. Chill. Yield: pastry for one 8-inch lattice-crust cobbler.

CRANBERRY PIE

Pastry for 1 double-crust (9-inch) pie
2½ cups sugar
½ cup all-purpose flour
2 cups water
5 cups fresh cranberries, halved
½ cup butter or margarine
2 teaspoons vanilla extract

Roll half of pastry to ⅛-inch thickness on a lightly floured surface; fit into a 9-inch pie-plate. Set aside. Chill remaining pastry.

Combine sugar and flour in a medium saucepan, mixing well. Add water; bring to a boil. Reduce heat; cook, stirring constantly, until thickened. Stir in cranberries, butter, and vanilla, mixing well. Spoon mixture evenly into pastry shell.

Roll remaining pastry to ⅛-inch thickness; cut into ¾-inch-wide strips, and arrange in a lattice design over filling. Seal and flute edges. Bake at 350° for 35 minutes or until browned. Yield: one 9-inch pie.

RASPBERRY PIE

½ cup currant jelly
1 tablespoon dark rum
4 cups fresh raspberries
1 baked (9-inch) pastry
  shell
Sweetened whipped cream

Combine currant jelly and rum in a small saucepan; mix well. Cook over medium heat, stirring frequently, just until mixture reaches a boil; cool completely.

Arrange raspberries evenly over bottom of pastry shell; drizzle jelly mixture over raspberries. Top with sweetened whipped cream before serving. Yield: one 9-inch pie.

PLANT CITY STRAWBERRY PIE

3½ pints strawberries,
  washed and hulled, divided
1 baked (9-inch) pastry shell
¾ cup sugar
½ cup water
2½ tablespoons cornstarch
1 tablespoon butter or
  margarine, softened
4 drops red food coloring
1 cup whipping cream
2 tablespoons superfine sugar
½ teaspoon vanilla extract
Fresh whole strawberries

Arrange 2½ pints strawberries in bottom of pastry shell; set aside.

Finely chop remaining strawberries, and place in a small saucepan. Add ¾ cup sugar, water, and cornstarch; stir well. Bring to a boil. Reduce heat and cook, stirring constantly, until thickened and bubbly.

Remove from heat, and stir in butter and food coloring. Cool slightly, and spoon mixture over strawberries in pastry shell. Chill thoroughly.

Before serving, combine whipping cream, superfine sugar, and vanilla in a medium mixing bowl; beat until soft peaks form. Pipe whipped cream onto pie. Garnish with whole strawberries. Yield: one 9-inch pie.

Strawberry packers at work, Plant City, Florida, 1930s.

OUR NATIVE HARVEST

Nut and Vegetable Pies

O f the many kinds of nut pies that appear on Southern tables, pecan is probably the most often served. Well, the big peanut-growing states in the neighborhood of Georgia and the Carolinas do consume a goodly number of peanut pies. Then there are the hickory nut and black walnut pies served where the hardwoods grow, in the Ozarks and the Appalachian country, but these nuts are not nearly so easy to come by as the pecan, which is one of the lower South's important cash crops.

No pie in the book is easier to make than a nut pie; it is simply a matter of finding the right combination of ingredients to pique the individual taste buds. Texans are torn between having their pecan pie with or without chocolate added. In Florida, they dote on the honey from the tupelo tree, claiming that it gives pecan pie a flavor like no other.

At the delightful old Wayside Inn in Middletown, Virginia, they use maple syrup instead of corn syrup or honey. Again, one must admit that it is among the richest combinations of flavors ever invented. Move on to Charleston, South Carolina, for a sample of the chocolate pecan pie that contains an irresistible hint of bourbon whiskey, and in Tennessee you can sample a spiced pecan-raisin pie with egg whites folded into the filling before baking.

Occasionally we encounter the problem of a nut pie over-browning in the oven. Herewith are two preventive measures: Bake the pie in the lower half of the oven. When reducing the heat after the first few minutes, put a sheet of aluminum foil over the upper oven shelf. Or put a little water in a baking pan on the upper shelf.

Texans make a Poor Man's Pecan Pie by using one-third cup of cornmeal and about half the usual quantity of pecans. But sweet economy, deeply ingrained in the heart of the South, is nowhere better represented than in our vegetable pies. Most familiar are pumpkin and sweet potato, popular since Mary Randolph's day. Others, such as bean, white potato, and green tomato, deserve wider exposure; they're delicious. By using vegetables as pie fillings, we can cut corners with no sacrifice in flavor. Do give them a try!

Here's a trio of pies seldom seen outside the South: Back to front are Peanut Pie (page 52), Mary Randolph's Sweet Potato Pie (page 57), and Green Tomato Pie (page 63) reminiscent of a green apple pie.

NUT PIES

PEANUT PIE

3 eggs, beaten
1 cup dark corn syrup
½ cup sugar
2 tablespoons butter or
  margarine, melted
1 teaspoon vanilla extract
1 cup salted peanuts
1 unbaked (9-inch) pastry
  shell

Combine eggs, syrup, sugar, butter, and vanilla in a medium mixing bowl; beat well. Stir in peanuts. Pour filling into pastry shell. Bake at 350° for 45 minutes or until set. Yield: one 9-inch pie.

*Peanut harvest time, from
an old stereograph.*

Library of Congress

ALABAMA PECAN PIE

1 cup sugar
1 tablespoon all-purpose flour
4 eggs, beaten
1 cup light corn syrup
1 tablespoon butter or
  margarine, melted
1 cup chopped pecans
1 unbaked (9-inch) pastry
  shell
¾ cup pecan halves

Combine sugar and flour in a large mixing bowl. Add eggs, syrup, and butter; beat well. Stir in chopped pecans. Pour mixture into pastry shell. Arrange pecan halves on top of pie. Bake at 350° for 55 minutes or until set. Yield: one 9-inch pie.

TUPELO HONEY PECAN PIE

½ cup butter or margarine,
  softened
1 cup sugar
3 eggs
¼ cup plus 2 tablespoons
  honey
3 tablespoons light corn
  syrup
¼ teaspoon salt
Pinch of baking soda
1 cup chopped pecans
1 unbaked (9-inch) pastry
  shell

Cream butter; gradually add sugar, beating well. Add eggs, one at a time, beating well after each addition.

Add honey, syrup, salt, and soda; beat well. Stir in pecans. Pour mixture into pastry shell. Bake at 375° for 30 minutes or until set. Yield: one 9-inch pie.

Note: If available, tupelo honey, which comes only from the tupelo tree in Florida, can be used in place of commercial honey.

TEXAS PECAN PIE

1 cup sugar
1 tablespoon all-purpose
  flour
⅛ teaspoon salt
4 eggs
½ cup light corn syrup
½ cup vegetable oil
1 teaspoon vanilla
  extract
1 cup chopped pecans
1 unbaked (9-inch) pastry
  shell

Combine sugar, flour, and salt in a medium mixing bowl. Add eggs, syrup, oil, and vanilla; beat at medium speed of an electric mixer until blended. Stir in pecans.

Pour mixture into pastry shell. Bake at 425° for 10 minutes. Reduce heat to 350°; bake 30 minutes or until filling is set. Yield: one 9-inch pie.

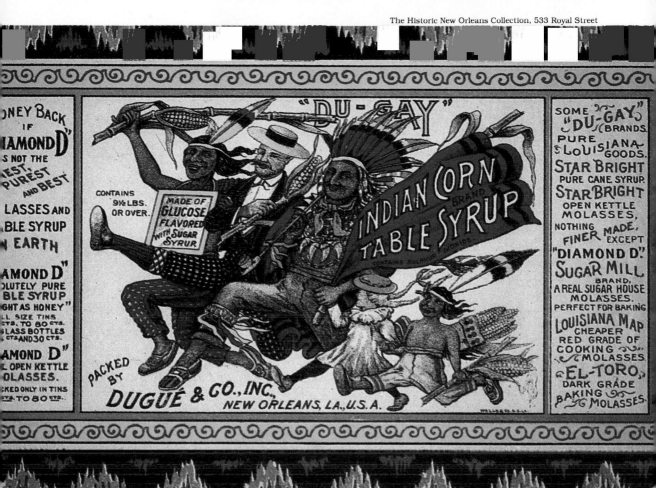

Exuberant celebration for Indian Corn Syrup. Early 1900s advertising label.

CHOCOLATE PECAN PIE

3 eggs, lightly beaten
1 cup sugar
1 cup light corn syrup
2 (1-ounce) squares unsweetened chocolate, melted
2 tablespoons butter or margarine, melted
1 cup pecan halves
1 teaspoon vanilla extract
Pinch of salt
1 unbaked (9-inch) pastry shell

Combine first 5 ingredients in a medium mixing bowl; mix well. Stir in pecans, vanilla, and salt. Pour mixture into pastry shell. Bake at 400° for 15 minutes. Reduce heat to 350°, and continue baking 30 minutes. Yield: one 9-inch pie.

The distinctive maple-flavored pecan pie is just one of the specials on the menu at The Wayside Inn, Middletown, Virginia. Serving an admiring public since 1797, Wayside Inn has adhered to the traditions of hospitality for which the Shenandoah Valley is famous. Waitresses in authentic eighteenth-century costume serve three meals a day the year 'round. Travelers often drive the 75 miles west out of Washington, D.C. to enjoy the restored inn's old-time atmosphere and fine foods.

WAYSIDE INN PECAN PIE

2 tablespoons butter or margarine, softened
½ cup firmly packed light brown sugar
1 cup maple syrup
1 tablespoon vanilla extract
3 eggs, beaten
2 cups coarsely chopped pecans
1 unbaked (9-inch) pastry shell

Combine butter, sugar, syrup, and vanilla in a medium mixing bowl. Add eggs, and beat well. Stir in pecans. Pour mixture into pastry shell. Bake at 325° for 1 hour or until set. Yield: one 9-inch pie.

Bourbon Chocolate Pecan Pie: They don't come much richer.

PECAN-RAISIN PIE

Pastry (recipe follows)
1 teaspoon sugar
2 eggs, separated
¾ cup sugar
½ teaspoon ground cloves
½ teaspoon ground cinnamon
½ teaspoon ground nutmeg
1 cup chopped pecans
½ cup golden raisins
¼ cup butter or margarine, melted
2 teaspoons white wine vinegar
1 cup whipping cream, whipped

Roll dough to ⅛-inch thickness on a lightly floured surface. Place in a 9-inch pieplate; trim edges. Fold edges under, and flute. Prick bottom and sides of shell with fork. Sprinkle bottom of pastry shell with 1 teaspoon sugar. Set aside.

Beat egg yolks in a medium mixing bowl until thick and lemon colored. Sift together ¾ cup sugar, cloves, cinnamon, and nutmeg; add to egg yolks, mixing well. Stir in pecans, raisins, and butter. Mix well.

Beat egg whites (at room temperature) until stiff peaks form. Gradually fold into pecan mixture, adding vinegar during folding process.

Pour pecan mixture into prepared pastry shell. Bake at 400° for 10 minutes. Reduce heat to 350°, and bake an additional 25 minutes. Cool slightly, and serve with whipped cream. Yield: one 9-inch pie.

Pastry:

1 cup all-purpose flour
½ teaspoon salt
⅓ cup shortening
2 to 3 tablespoons cold milk

Combine flour and salt in a mixing bowl. Cut in shortening with a pastry blender until mixture resembles coarse meal. Stir in enough milk, 1 tablespoon at a time, to moisten dry ingredients. Turn onto a lightly floured surface, and knead gently to form a smooth ball. Chill dough 1 hour. Yield: pastry for one 9-inch pie.

BOURBON CHOCOLATE PECAN PIE

3 eggs
¼ cup plus 2 tablespoons butter or margarine, melted
¾ cup light corn syrup
½ cup sugar
¼ cup firmly packed brown sugar
2 tablespoons bourbon
1 tablespoon all-purpose flour
1 teaspoon vanilla extract
1 cup chopped pecans
1 cup semisweet chocolate morsels
1 unbaked (9-inch) pastry shell

Beat eggs in a large mixing bowl until frothy. Add butter, beating well. Add syrup, sugar, bourbon, flour, and vanilla; beat well. Stir in pecans.

Sprinkle chocolate morsels in pastry shell. Pour pecan mixture over chocolate morsels. Bake at 350° for 1 hour or until set. Cool before slicing. Yield: one 9-inch pie.

TEXAS POOR BOY PIE

1⅔ cups sugar
⅓ cup white cornmeal
Pinch of salt
4 eggs, well beaten
½ cup butter or margarine, melted
⅓ cup milk
2 teaspoons vanilla extract
¼ cup chopped pecans
1 unbaked (9-inch) pastry shell
Pecan halves

Combine first 7 ingredients in a medium mixing bowl; beat well. Stir in chopped pecans. Pour filling into pastry shell. Top with pecan halves. Bake at 350° for 55 minutes or until set. Cool before slicing. Yield: one 9-inch pie.

BLACK WALNUT PIE

¼ cup plus 2 tablespoons butter or margarine, softened
¾ cup sugar
½ cup firmly packed brown sugar
4 eggs
½ cup whipping cream
¼ cup light corn syrup
¼ teaspoon salt
¾ cup chopped black walnuts
1 teaspoon vanilla extract
1 unbaked (9-inch) pastry shell
Whipped cream (optional)

Cream butter in top of a double boiler; gradually add sugar, beating well. Add eggs, one at a time, beating well after each addition. Add whipping cream, syrup, and salt, beating well.

Place over rapidly boiling water and cook, stirring constantly, 5 minutes or until mixture thickens. Stir in walnuts and vanilla.

Pour filling into pastry shell. Bake at 350° for 45 minutes or until set. Cool and serve with whipped cream, if desired. Yield: one 9-inch pie.

Note: ¾ cup chopped hickory nuts may be substituted for chopped walnuts.

Shaking ripe pecans from the trees in Flemington, Georgia, in the fall of 1908.

VEGETABLE PIES

OKLAHOMA BEAN PIE

1 (16-ounce) can navy beans,
  drained and pureed
3 eggs, beaten
¾ cup sugar
2 teaspoons vanilla extract
Pinch of salt
1 unbaked (9-inch) pastry
  shell

Combine beans, eggs, sugar, vanilla, and salt in a medium mixing bowl; beat well. Pour mixture into pastry shell. Bake at 350° for 45 minutes or until a knife inserted in center comes out clean. Cool pie before serving. Yield: one 9-inch pie.

MARYLAND WHITE POTATO PIE

2 medium potatoes, cooked,
  peeled, and mashed
⅔ cup butter or margarine
1 cup sugar
½ teaspoon baking powder
⅛ teaspoon salt
½ cup whipping cream
½ cup milk
2 teaspoons grated lemon
  rind
2 tablespoons lemon juice
1 teaspoon vanilla extract
⅛ teaspoon ground nutmeg
4 eggs, beaten
1 unbaked (9-inch) pastry
  shell

Combine potatoes, butter, sugar, baking powder, and salt in a medium mixing bowl; mix well. Gradually add whipping cream and milk, stirring until well blended. Stir in lemon rind, juice, vanilla, and nutmeg. Add eggs; mix well.

Pour mixture into pastry shell; bake at 350° for 55 minutes or until a knife inserted in center comes out clean. Cool. Yield: one 9-inch pie.

Maryland White Potato Pie, a long cherished Southern tradition.

MARY RANDOLPH'S SWEET POTATO PIE

¼ cup butter or margarine,
  softened
1 cup sugar
2 cups cooked, mashed sweet
  potatoes
3 eggs
¼ cup brandy
2 teaspoons grated lemon
  rind
2 tablespoons lemon juice
1 teaspoon vanilla extract
Dash of ground nutmeg
1 unbaked (9-inch) pastry
  shell
Finely chopped citron

Cream butter in a mixing bowl; gradually add sugar, beating well. Add potatoes; beat at medium speed of electric mixer until well blended. Add eggs, one at a time, beating well after each addition.

Place brandy in a small pan; heat just until warm (do not boil). Add brandy, lemon rind, juice, vanilla, and nutmeg to sweet potato mixture; stir until well blended.

Pour mixture into pastry shell. Bake at 350° for 40 minutes or until a knife inserted in center comes out clean. Sprinkle pie with citron; cool completely. Yield: one 9-inch pie.

1894 SWEET POTATO PIE

2 medium-size sweet
  potatoes
1 recipe Puff Paste
  (see page 18)
½ cup sugar
½ cup water
½ cup butter or margarine,
  melted
¼ teaspoon ground cinnamon
⅛ teaspoon ground allspice
⅛ teaspoon ground cloves

Cook sweet potatoes in boiling water 10 minutes; let cool to touch. Peel and cut into ¼-inch-thick slices; set aside.

Roll half of pastry to ⅛-inch thickness on a lightly floured surface. Carefully fit into a 9-inch pieplate. Chill remaining pastry. Arrange sweet potato slices evenly in the pastry shell, and set aside.

Combine sugar, water, butter, and spices; stir well. Pour mixture over sweet potatoes.

Roll out remaining pastry to ⅛-inch thickness on a lightly floured surface, and place over filling. Trim edges; seal and flute. Cut slits in top pastry to allow steam to escape. Bake at 325° for 50 minutes or until golden brown. Cool pie before serving. Yield: one 9-inch pie.

Lowly ingredients never deterred the Southern cook from having a pie when the family clamored for one. Pies utilizing beans or Irish potatoes sometimes have "Poor Man's . . ." in the title, but sweet potatoes were used without apology of any kind. Oatmeal, substituted for pecans, gave body to an old-fashioned Poor Man's Pecan Pie. Vinegar or buttermilk gave tartness to non-lemon pies on occasion. Our vegetable pie tradition reaches back to England, but sweet potato, pumpkin, and squash pies must be labeled "Made in America."

VIRGINIA SWEET POTATO-PECAN PIE

1½ cups cooked, mashed
  sweet potatoes
½ cup firmly packed light
  brown sugar
1 teaspoon ground
  cinnamon
1 teaspoon ground
  ginger
¼ teaspoon salt
1½ cups milk, scalded
2 eggs, beaten
1 unbaked (9-inch) pastry
  shell
¼ cup butter or margarine
½ cup firmly packed light
  brown sugar
¾ cup chopped pecans
Whipped cream (optional)

Combine sweet potatoes, ½
cup sugar, cinnamon, ginger,
salt, and milk; mix well. Cook
until thoroughly heated. Gradually stir about one-fourth of hot
mixture into eggs; add to remaining hot mixture, stirring
constantly. Spoon into pastry
shell. Bake at 350° for 20 minutes. Remove from oven.
Cream butter and ½ cup
sugar; stir in pecans. Sprinkle
pecan mixture over pie; continue baking 45 minutes. Cool.
Serve with whipped cream, if
desired. Yield: one 9-inch pie.

SWEET POTATO-COCONUT PIE

5 eggs, beaten
2 cups sugar
2¼ cups milk
2 cups cooked, mashed sweet
  potatoes
¼ cup butter or margarine,
  melted
Dash of salt
1 tablespoon vanilla
  extract
½ teaspoon lemon extract
2 unbaked (9-inch) pastry
  shells
½ cup flaked coconut

Combine eggs and sugar in a
medium mixing bowl; beat well.
Add milk, mixing thoroughly.
Combine sweet potatoes, butter, salt, and flavorings. Add to
egg mixture; mix well.
Pour mixture into pastry
shells. Sprinkle ¼ cup coconut
over each pie. Bake at 375° for 1
hour or until set. Cool. Yield:
two 9-inch pies.

Andrew Jackson's Her-
mitage, twelve miles
from Nashville, is a
shrine to one of the South's
monumental heroes. Born in
1767 and orphaned before
the age of 14, Jackson had a
tenacious sense of family
duty which extended to the
relatives of his bride, Rachel
Robards. He built the first
Hermitage, a log house, for
Rachel in 1804. In 1818, he
began the present mansion,
to which he retired upon
leaving the White House.

GRANDMOTHER'S SWEET POTATO COBBLER

1 cup sugar
2 tablespoons cornstarch
1 teaspoon ground nutmeg
⅛ teaspoon salt
1 cup milk
1 tablespoon vinegar
¾ teaspoon yellow food
  coloring
1 teaspoon vanilla extract
1 tablespoon butter or
  margarine
6 cups cooked, chopped
  sweet potatoes
Pastry for a 9-inch pie

Combine sugar, cornstarch,
nutmeg, and salt in a saucepan;
set aside. Combine milk, vinegar, food coloring, vanilla, and
butter; add to sugar mixture,
and bring to a boil. Reduce heat,
and cook 1 minute, stirring constantly. Add sweet potatoes;
cook until thoroughly heated.
Spoon mixture into a lightly
greased 10- x 6- x 2-inch baking
dish. Roll pastry on a lightly
floured surface to fit the top of
the baking dish. Place over top
of dish, and seal edges. Make
slits in top of pastry to allow
steam to escape. Bake at 375°
for 40 minutes or until golden
brown. Cool before serving.
Yield: 8 servings.

*Coconut label,
c.1900.*

This 1856 lithograph takes in The Hermitage, Jackson's tomb, and A.J. Donelson's residence.

HERMITAGE SWEET POTATO-PUMPKIN PIE

Pastry (recipe follows)
1 cup firmly packed brown sugar
½ cup dark corn syrup
3 eggs, beaten
2 teaspoons ground cinnamon
½ teaspoon ground nutmeg
¼ teaspoon ground ginger
¼ teaspoon ground cloves
¼ teaspoon salt
1 cup cooked, mashed sweet potatoes
1 cup cooked, mashed pumpkin
2 tablespoons dark rum
1 teaspoon vanilla extract
1 (13-ounce) can evaporated milk
½ cup whipping cream
1 tablespoon sugar
Additional ground cinnamon

Roll chilled pastry to ⅛-inch thickness on a lightly floured surface. Place in a 10-inch deep-dish pieplate; trim excess pastry. Fold edges under, and flute. Set aside.

Combine sugar, syrup, eggs, spices, and salt in a large mixing bowl, beating well. Stir in sweet potatoes, pumpkin, rum, vanilla, and milk.

Pour pumpkin mixture into prepared pastry shell. Bake at 350° for 1 hour and 15 minutes or until set. Cool pie to room temperature.

Beat whipping cream until foamy; gradually add sugar, beating until soft peaks form. Garnish with whipped cream; sprinkle with additional cinnamon. Yield: one 10-inch pie.

Pastry:

1½ cups all-purpose flour
½ teaspoon salt
½ cup shortening
4 to 5 tablespoons cold water

Combine flour and salt; cut in shortening until mixture resembles coarse meal. Sprinkle water evenly over surface; stir with a fork until dry ingredients are moistened. Shape dough into a ball; chill. Yield: pastry for one 10-inch deep-dish pie.

83N-2 PLAYING COOK

VIRGINIA PUMPKIN PIE

2 (16-ounce) cans pumpkin
2 cups sugar
4 eggs, separated
2 cups milk
2 teaspoons ground cinnamon
½ teaspoon ground nutmeg
¼ teaspoon ground cloves
¼ teaspoon salt
2 teaspoons vanilla extract
Pastry (recipes follows)

Combine pumpkin, sugar, egg yolks, milk, cinnamon, nutmeg, cloves, salt, and vanilla in a medium mixing bowl. Beat at medium speed of an electric mixer 1 minute or until smooth.

Beat egg whites (at room temperature) until soft peaks form. Fold whites into pumpkin mixture. Pour equal amounts of filling into prepared pastry shells. Bake at 350° for 40 minutes or until knife inserted in center comes out clean. Cool before slicing. Yield: two 9-inch pies.

Pastry:

2⅔ cups all-purpose flour
1 teaspoon salt
⅔ cup vegetable oil
¼ cup plus 2 tablespoons milk

Combine flour and salt; mix well. Combine oil and milk (do not stir). With a fork, stir in liquid to moisten dry ingredients. Divide dough in half; shape into two balls and chill.

Roll each portion of dough to ⅛-inch thickness on a lightly floured surface. Place in two 9-inch pieplates; flute edges. Prick bottoms and sides of shells. Bake at 475° for 10 minutes or until golden brown. Cool. Yield: two 9-inch pastry shells.

Illustration from cover of a recipe booklet published by a baking powder company, 1920, shows a rather professional-looking group of little helpers intent on baking pies.

Advertising card boasts, "We grow pumpkins like this."

PUMPKIN MERINGUE PIE

¾ cup sugar
2 tablespoons all-purpose flour
½ teaspoon ground cinnamon
½ teaspoon ground nutmeg
¼ teaspoon ground ginger
1 cup cooked, mashed pumpkin
2 tablespoons butter or margarine, melted
3 eggs, separated
1 cup evaporated milk
1 teaspoon vanilla extract
1 unbaked (9-inch) pastry shell
¼ cup plus 2 tablespoons sugar

Combine first 5 ingredients in a medium mixing bowl; add pumpkin and butter. Combine egg yolks, milk, and vanilla; add to pumpkin mixture, mixing well. Pour filling into pastry shell. Bake at 350° for 45 minutes or until knife inserted in center comes out clean.

Beat egg whites (at room temperature) until foamy. Gradually add ¼ cup plus 2 tablespoons sugar, 1 tablespoon at a time, beating until stiff peaks form. Spread meringue over filling, sealing to edge of pastry. Bake at 350° for 12 minutes or until meringue is golden brown. Cool to room temperature before serving. Yield: one 9-inch pie.

PUMPKIN-PECAN PIE

1½ cups sugar
1½ teaspoons all-purpose flour
1½ teaspoons ground cinnamon
¾ teaspoon ground nutmeg
¾ teaspoon salt
1½ cups cooked, mashed pumpkin
2 eggs
1½ cups milk
¾ cup chopped pecans
1 unbaked (9-inch) pastry shell

Combine first 5 ingredients; mix well. Add pumpkin, eggs, and milk, stirring until well blended. Stir in pecans.

Pour filling into pastry shell. Bake at 350° for 45 minutes or until a knife inserted in center comes out clean. Cool before serving. Yield: one 9-inch pie.

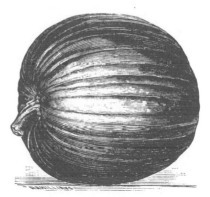

Texas folk artist Eva McDaniel Jones' evocative rendition of Harvest Time. *Below:* Whiskey Label, c.1800.

Collection of Business Americana

BOURBON-PUMPKIN PIE

2 tablespoons butter or margarine, softened
¾ cup sugar
3 eggs
1 cup cooked, mashed pumpkin
1 cup evaporated milk
2 tablespoons bourbon, heated
½ teaspoon salt
¼ teaspoon ground ginger
¼ teaspoon ground nutmeg
¼ teaspoon ground cinnamon
1 unbaked (9-inch) pastry shell

Cream butter and sugar in a medium mixing bowl; add eggs, one at a time, beating well after each addition. Combine pumpkin, milk, bourbon, salt, ginger, nutmeg, and cinnamon. Add pumpkin mixture to egg mixture, mixing well.

Pour filling into pastry shell. Bake at 450° for 10 minutes. Reduce heat to 325°, and continue baking 45 minutes or until a knife inserted in center comes out clean. Cool before serving. Yield: one 9-inch pie.

BUTTERNUT SQUASH PIE

1 cup cooked, mashed butternut squash
¾ cup milk, scalded
⅓ cup sugar
⅓ cup firmly packed light brown sugar
2 eggs, beaten
¾ teaspoon ground cinnamon
¼ teaspoon ground nutmeg
¼ teaspoon salt
1 unbaked (9-inch) pastry shell
¾ cup finely chopped pecans
½ cup firmly packed light brown sugar
¼ cup butter or margarine, softened
Whipped cream

Combine squash, milk, sugar, ⅓ cup brown sugar, eggs, cinnamon, nutmeg, and salt in a large mixing bowl; beat well. Pour mixture into pastry shell. Bake at 375° for 20 minutes. Remove from oven.

Combine pecans, ½ cup sugar, and butter; mix well. Sprinkle mixture over top of pie. Bake at 375° an additional 25 minutes. Cool slightly, and serve with whipped cream. Yield: one 9-inch pie.

YELLOW SQUASH PIE

5 eggs, separated
3 cups cooked, mashed yellow squash
⅔ cup sugar
½ cup evaporated milk
1 tablespoon all-purpose flour
1 tablespoon butter or margarine, melted
2 teaspoons vanilla extract
½ teaspoon ground cinnamon
¼ teaspoon salt
1 baked (9-inch) pastry shell
Ground nutmeg
½ teaspoon cream of tartar
½ cup plus 2 tablespoons sugar

Beat egg yolks in a Dutch oven until thick and lemon colored. Add next 8 ingredients; mix well. Cook over medium heat until thickened. Pour mixture into pastry shell. Sprinkle with nutmeg.

Beat egg whites (at room temperature) and cream of tartar until foamy. Gradually add remaining sugar, one tablespoon at a time, beating until stiff peaks form. Spread over hot filling, sealing to edge of pastry. Bake at 350° for 10 minutes or until golden brown. Cool. Yield: one 9-inch pie.

GREEN TOMATO PIE

Pastry for 1 double-crust (9-inch) pie
1 cup sugar
¾ cup water
6 small green tomatoes, thinly sliced
2 teaspoons grated lemon rind
¾ teaspoon ground cinnamon
½ cup raisins

Roll half of pastry to ⅛-inch thickness on a lightly floured surface; fit into a 9-inch pie-plate. Set aside.

Combine sugar and water in a medium saucepan. Cook over low heat until sugar dissolves, stirring occasionally. Add tomatoes; cook over medium heat 5 minutes, stirring frequently. Stir in lemon rind and cinnamon; continue cooking 15 minutes or until thickened, stirring frequently. Stir in raisins. Remove from heat, and cool slightly. Pour into pastry shell.

Roll remaining pastry to ⅛-inch thickness. Cut into ¾-inch-wide strips; arrange in a lattice fashion over filling. Trim edges; seal and flute. Bake at 375° for 35 minutes. Yield: one 9-inch pie.

OLD-WORLD HERITAGE

Custard, Chess, and Cheese Pies

For purposes of organization, the recipes in this chapter on custard pies, with subdivisions of chess and cheese pies, are defined as those in which the filling is mixed, poured into unbaked pie shells, and then baked together. To illustrate: In Mary F. Henderson's 1887 *Practical Cooking and Dinner Giving*, there is a certain lemon pie. The filling is cooked, poured into baked crusts, meringue applied, and "put into the oven a few minutes to color." This would appear in our cream pie section. Conversely, her orange pie filling is mixed up raw and the egg whites folded in. Then she says, "Bake in paste-lined pie-plates." This recipe would go into the present chapter. It is similar to our Lee Family Orange Pie, except that in the latter, the meringue is on top.

To use the traditional definition of custard as milk or cream with only eggs for thickening would be to restrict ourselves unduly; there are many good pies baked filling-in-shell. Here we place the classic chess pie. In Kentucky, chess pies are sometimes baked, all but the bottom crust rimless, and stacked sometimes six-deep to be transported to an outing. Dangerously rich, the chess pie.

The main advantage in baking filling with crust is the saving in time. There is a drawback, however: Unless steps are taken, the crust can come out sodden instead of crisp. This problem may be obviated in any of several ways: Before adding the filling, prick tiny holes in the crust and blind-bake (pre-bake) it for five minutes or so, long enough to set it but not brown it. Better still, brush it with slightly beaten egg white; then prick holes and blind-bake. This seals the crust against moisture.

Addressing basic custard pie another way, some cooks bake the crust empty, pour the custard into a matching pie-pan, buttered, and bake it separately in a shallow pan of water. This is called "slip custard pie" because, after baking, the custard is loosened around the edge and "slipped" into the baked crust. No, it isn't all that difficult to do!

From unctuous plain custard to multi-ingredient combinations, the pies in this collection are fine eating.

Four Southern favorites photographed in the old kitchen at the Hermitage, Nashville (clockwise from front): Hermitage Chess Pie (page 72), James K. Polk's Vinegar Pie (page 77), Tennessee Lemon Chess Pie (page 74), and Mary's Buttermilk Pie (page 66).

BASIC CUSTARD PIES

MARY'S BUTTERMILK PIE

1 cup butter or margarine, melted
3 cups sugar
6 eggs
¼ cup all-purpose flour
1 cup buttermilk
2 tablespoons water
1 teaspoon vanilla extract
½ teaspoon lemon juice
2 unbaked (9-inch) pastry shells

Combine butter, sugar, eggs, flour, buttermilk, and water in a medium mixing bowl; beat well. Stir in vanilla and lemon juice; mix well.

Pour filling evenly into pastry shells. Bake at 350° for 50 minutes or until a knife inserted in center comes out clean. Cool pies before slicing. Yield: two 9-inch pies.

Buttermilk has always been one of the South's staple ingredients, and it will come as no surprise to find buttermilk custard pie here in two versions. The German recipe has egg white folded in to form a sponge-like top layer.

"Mrs. Doc's" pies were favorite treats for forty years in Guntersville, Alabama, where Mr. and Mrs. Doc Cornelius (center) reigned as restaurateurs.

GERMAN BUTTERMILK PIE

1¼ cups sugar
3 tablespoons all-purpose flour
¼ teaspoon salt
3 eggs, separated
2 cups buttermilk
¼ cup butter or margarine, melted
¼ teaspoon cream of tartar
1 unbaked (10-inch) pastry shell

Combine sugar, flour, and salt in a large mixing bowl; stir well. Add egg yolks, buttermilk, and butter; beat well.

Beat egg whites (at room temperature) and cream of tartar until stiff peaks form. Fold into buttermilk mixture. Pour filling into pastry shell. Bake at 375° for 45 minutes or until a knife inserted in center comes out clean. Yield: one 10-inch pie.

Chocolate Lover's Fudge Pie temptingly topped with ice cream.

MRS. DOC'S EGG CUSTARD PIE

3 eggs, beaten
¾ cup sugar
1 tablespoon all-purpose flour
1 tablespoon cornstarch
1 teaspoon vanilla extract
1¾ cups milk
1 unbaked (9-inch) pastry shell
2 tablespoons butter or margarine
½ teaspoon ground nutmeg

Preheat oven to 500°.
Combine eggs, sugar, flour, cornstarch, and vanilla in a medium mixing bowl; beat until smooth. Add milk, and stir until well blended. Pour mixture into pastry shell; dot with butter, and sprinkle with nutmeg.
Place pie in preheated oven, immediately reduce temperature to 350°. Bake 45 minutes or until a knife inserted in center comes out clean. Cool before slicing. Yield: one 9-inch pie.

EGG CUSTARD MERINGUE PIE

4 eggs, separated
1 cup sugar
1 tablespoon all-purpose flour
¼ cup butter or margarine, melted
1 cup milk
1 teaspoon vanilla extract
⅛ teaspoon ground nutmeg
1 unbaked (9-inch) pastry shell
½ teaspoon cream of tartar
½ cup sugar
1 teaspoon vanilla extract

Place egg yolks in a large mixing bowl; beat until frothy. Add 1 cup sugar, flour, and butter; beat well. Stir in milk, 1 teaspoon vanilla, and nutmeg. Pour mixture into pastry shell. Bake at 325° for 50 minutes or until a knife inserted in center comes out clean.
Beat egg whites (at room temperature) and cream of tartar until foamy. Gradually add ½ cup sugar, 1 tablespoon at a time, beating until stiff peaks form and sugar dissolves. Beat in 1 teaspoon vanilla. Spread meringue over filling, sealing to edge of pastry. Bake at 350° for 10 minutes or until meringue is lightly browned. Cool before serving. Yield: one 9-inch pie.

CHOCOLATE LOVER'S FUDGE PIE

1 cup sugar
3 eggs
½ cup light corn syrup
½ cup evaporated milk
½ cup cocoa
3 tablespoons butter or margarine, melted
¼ teaspoon salt
1 teaspoon vanilla extract
1 unbaked (9-inch) pastry shell
Vanilla ice cream

Combine first 8 ingredients in a medium mixing bowl; beat well. Pour mixture into pastry shell. Bake at 375° for 40 minutes or until a knife inserted in center comes out clean. Serve warm with ice cream. Yield: one 9-inch pie.

FRENCH HUGUENOT CHOCOLATE PIE

¼ cup butter or margarine, melted
1½ (1-ounce) squares unsweetened chocolate, melted and cooled
1½ cups sugar
1 tablespoon all-purpose flour
2 eggs
½ cup milk
1 teaspoon vanilla extract
Dash of salt
1 unbaked (9-inch) pastry shell

Combine first 8 ingredients; beat 5 minutes at medium speed of electric mixer. Pour into pastry shell. Bake at 400° for 10 minutes. Reduce temperature to 350°; bake 40 minutes. Cool. Yield: one 9-inch pie.

Chocolate comes in bars, bits, or powdered.
Advertising card, 1800s.

PLEASANT HILL CHOCOLATE MORSEL PIE

¼ cup butter or margarine
1 cup sugar
3 eggs, beaten
¾ cup light corn syrup
¼ teaspoon salt
1 teaspoon vanilla extract
½ cup semisweet chocolate morsels
½ cup chopped pecans
2 tablespoons bourbon
1 unbaked (9-inch) pastry shell

Cream butter; gradually add sugar, beating well. Add eggs, syrup, salt, and vanilla; beat well. Stir in chocolate morsels, pecans, and bourbon. Pour mixture into pastry shell.

Bake at 375° for 40 minutes or until a knife inserted in center comes out clean. Cool slightly before serving. Yield: one 9-inch pie.

NO-CRUST FUDGE PIE

3 (1-ounce) squares unsweetened chocolate
½ cup butter or margarine
3 eggs, beaten
1½ cups sugar
¼ cup all-purpose flour
1 teaspoon milk
½ teaspoon salt
½ teaspoon vanilla extract
Vanilla ice cream (optional)

Combine chocolate and butter in top of a double boiler; cook over boiling water until melted, stirring occasionally. Remove from heat; cool.

Add chocolate mixture to eggs; beat well. Add sugar, flour, milk, salt, and vanilla; beat until well blended. Pour mixture into a well-greased 9-inch pie-plate. Bake at 325° for 50 minutes. Serve warm with vanilla ice cream, if desired. Yield: one 9-inch pie.

MARION FLEXNER'S APPLE CUSTARD PIE

1 cup sugar
¼ cup water
2 tablespoons butter or
  margarine
1 teaspoon ground cinnamon
¼ teaspoon ground nutmeg
5 medium-size baking apples,
  peeled, cored, and sliced
1 unbaked (9-inch) pastry
  shell
1 egg, beaten
1 tablespoon all-purpose flour
⅔ cup whipping cream

Combine sugar, water, butter, cinnamon, and nutmeg in a medium Dutch oven; stir well. Cook over medium heat, stirring occasionally, until butter melts. Add apples; cover and cook 10 minutes or until apples are tender. Drain apples, reserving ½ cup syrup.

Arrange apple slices in pastry shell; pour syrup over apple slices. Bake at 450° for 5 minutes. Reduce heat to 375°, and bake an additional 15 minutes. Remove pie from oven.

Combine egg and flour in a small mixing bowl, stirring until well blended. Gradually add whipping cream, stirring until smooth. Pour over apple slices. Return pie to oven, and bake at 375° an additional 10 minutes. Cool before slicing. Yield: one 9-inch pie.

Marion Flexner's *Out of Kentucky Kitchens*, 1949, is considered the definitive Kentucky cookbook. The Alabama born, Wellesley-educated woman moved to Louisville where she married Dr. Morris Flexner. A woman of broad interests ranging from fishing to cooking, gardening, and writing for juveniles, she published her first cookbook, *Dixie Dishes*, in the year 1941.

Marion Flexner's Apple Custard Pie will make your day.

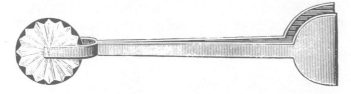

DEWBERRY CUSTARD PIE

4 cups fresh dewberries
1 unbaked (10-inch) pastry
   shell
2 eggs, beaten
1½ cups sugar
½ cup all-purpose flour
½ cup whipping cream
¼ cup plus 2 tablespoons
   all-purpose flour
¼ cup plus 2 tablespoons
   sugar
3 tablespoons butter or
   margarine

Place berries in pastry shell.
Set aside.

Combine eggs, 1½ cups sugar, ½ cup flour, and whipping cream in a medium mixing bowl; beat well. Pour mixture over berries.

Combine ¼ cup plus 2 tablespoons flour and ¼ cup plus 2 tablespoons sugar in a small mixing bowl. Cut in butter with a pastry blender until mixture resembles coarse meal. Sprinkle mixture over filling. Bake at 325° for 1 hour and 15 minutes or until lightly browned. Cool before serving. Yield: one 10-inch pie.

FLORIDA LIME CUSTARD PIE

5 egg yolks
1 (14-ounce) can sweetened
   condensed milk
½ teaspoon grated lime rind
⅔ cup lime juice
3 egg whites
1 baked (9-inch) pastry shell
1 cup whipping cream
2 tablespoons sugar
½ teaspoon vanilla extract

Beat yolks until thick and lemon colored. Gradually add milk, beating constantly. Add lime rind and juice; mix well.

Beat egg whites (at room temperature) until stiff peaks form. Gently fold whites into lime mixture. Spoon mixture into pastry shell. Bake at 325° for 25 minutes. Cool to room temperature. Chill at least 3 hours. (Pie will set upon cooling.)

Beat whipping cream until foamy. Gradually add sugar, beating until soft peaks form. Stir in vanilla. Garnish top of pie with whipped cream before serving. Yield: one 9-inch pie.

SOUR CREAM-RAISIN PIE

3 eggs
1½ cups sugar
1 (8-ounce) carton
   commercial sour cream
1 cup raisins
½ cup chopped pecans
1 unbaked (9-inch) pastry
   shell

Beat eggs in a medium mixing bowl until thick and lemon colored. Stir in sugar. Add sour cream, raisins, and pecans; blend well. Pour into pastry shell. Bake at 400° for 10 minutes. Reduce temperature to 350°; bake 45 minutes. Cool. Yield: one 9-inch pie.

Dewberry: The name for a trailing bramble that bears sweet edible berries related to and resembling blackberries.

A picnic in Davenport, Florida, c.1910, being photographed by smiling picnicker on right.

OLD-FASHIONED COCONUT CUSTARD PIE

1½ cups sugar
2 eggs
½ teaspoon salt
½ cup butter or margarine, melted
¼ cup all-purpose flour
½ cup milk
1½ cups flaked coconut, divided
1 unbaked (9-inch) pastry shell

Combine sugar, eggs, and salt in a medium mixing bowl; beat until light and lemon colored. Combine butter and flour, stirring until well blended. Add flour mixture to egg mixture; beat well. Gradually add milk, beating until smooth and creamy. Fold in 1 cup coconut.

Pour mixture into unbaked pastry shell. Sprinkle remaining ½ cup coconut over top. Bake at 325° for 1 hour and 10 minutes or until a knife inserted in center comes out clean. Cool slightly before serving. Yield: one 9-inch pie.

CHESS PIES AND VARIATIONS

REBECCA BOONE'S CHESS PIE

5 eggs, beaten
1½ cups sugar
1 tablespoon cornmeal
¼ cup plus 2 tablespoons
   butter or margarine, melted
1 tablespoon vinegar
1 teaspoon vanilla extract
1 unbaked (9-inch) pastry
   shell

Combine first 3 ingredients; beat well. Add butter, vinegar, and vanilla, beating well. Pour into pastry shell. Bake at 350° for 50 minutes. Cool before slicing. Yield: one 9-inch pie.

Daniel Boone Escorting a Band of Pioneers into the Western Country in 1775, *by George Caleb Bingham.*

Daniel Boone, a native of Pennsylvania, moved to North Carolina at age 16. Intrigued by John Finley's *Tales of Kentucky*, he penetrated the Bluegrass in the late 1760s. Indians turned back his first colonizing effort, but he and 30 armed men came back in 1775 along the Wilderness Trail, blazing it as they went. Fort Boonesboro was built, and other settlers followed. However, Boone did not bring his wife, Rebecca, until the frontier had calmed down somewhat.

HERMITAGE CHESS PIE

2 cups sugar
2 tablespoons cornmeal
2 tablespoons all-purpose
   flour
½ cup butter or margarine,
   softened
1 cup milk
5 egg yolks
1 unbaked (9-inch) pastry
   shell

Combine first 3 ingredients; mix well. Set aside.

Cream butter in a medium mixing bowl; add sugar mixture, beating well. Add milk and yolks. Pour into pastry shell. Bake at 425° for 15 minutes. Reduce heat to 375°, and continue baking 45 minutes. Cool before slicing. Yield: one 9-inch pie.

CHOCOLATE CHESS PIE

1½ cups sugar
¼ cup cocoa
Pinch of salt
2 eggs
¼ cup butter or margarine, melted
1 (5.33-ounce) can evaporated milk
1 teaspoon vanilla extract
1 unbaked (9-inch) pastry shell

Combine sugar, cocoa, and salt; stir well. Set aside.

Combine eggs, butter, milk, and vanilla in a mixing bowl; beat well. Add sugar mixture; mix well. Pour filling into pastry shell. Bake at 350° for 45 to 50 minutes. Cool before slicing. Yield: one 9-inch pie.

BROWN SUGAR CHESS PIE

4 eggs
2 cups firmly packed brown sugar
⅔ cup whipping cream
½ cup butter or margarine, melted
1 unbaked (9-inch) pastry shell

Combine eggs, sugar, whipping cream, and butter; beat well. Pour into pastry shell. Bake at 350° for 50 minutes or until a knife inserted in center comes out clean. Cool before slicing. Yield: one 9-inch pie.

Chocolate Chess Pie (front) and Chess Meringue Pie (rear)

CHESS MERINGUE PIE

1 egg
3 eggs, separated
1 cup sugar
½ cup firmly packed light brown sugar
3 tablespoons all-purpose flour
1 tablespoon cornmeal
¼ cup butter or margarine, melted
¼ cup milk
1 teaspoon vanilla extract
½ teaspoon vinegar
1 unbaked (9-inch) pastry shell
¼ teaspoon cream of tartar
¼ cup plus 2 tablespoons sugar

Combine 1 egg and 3 egg yolks in a medium mixing bowl; beat slightly. Combine 1 cup sugar, brown sugar, flour, and cornmeal, mixing well; add to egg mixture, mixing until smooth. Add butter, milk, vanilla, and vinegar; mix well. Pour filling into pastry shell. Bake at 400° for 10 minutes. Reduce heat to 325°, and continue baking 45 minutes.

Beat egg whites (at room temperature) until foamy; add cream of tartar, beating slightly. Gradually add remaining sugar, 1 tablespoon at a time, beating until stiff peaks form and sugar dissolves. Spread meringue over hot filling, sealing to edge of pastry. Bake at 350° for 10 minutes or until meringue is golden brown. Yield: one 9-inch pie.

TENNESSEE LEMON CHESS PIE

4 eggs, lightly beaten
2 cups sugar
1 tablespoon all-purpose flour
1 tablespoon cornmeal
¼ cup milk
¼ cup butter or margarine, melted
2 teaspoons grated lemon rind
¼ cup lemon juice
1 unbaked (9-inch) pastry shell

Combine eggs and sugar; beat well. Add flour and cornmeal, mixing until well blended. Add milk, butter, lemon rind, and juice; beat well. Pour filling into pastry shell. Bake at 375° for 55 minutes or until a knife inserted in center comes out clean. Cool before slicing. Yield: one 9-inch pie.

PECAN CHESS PIE

½ cup butter or margarine, softened
1 cup sugar
¼ cup all-purpose flour
⅛ teaspoon salt
3 egg yolks
1 (5.33-ounce) can evaporated milk
1 teaspoon vanilla extract
1 unbaked (9-inch) pastry shell
⅔ cup coarsely chopped pecans

Cream butter in a medium mixing bowl; gradually add sugar, beating well. Add flour, salt, and egg yolks; mix well. Stir in milk and vanilla. Pour filling into pastry shell; sprinkle with pecans. Bake at 425° for 10 minutes. Reduce heat to 300°, and bake an additional 35 minutes. Cool before slicing. Yield: one 9-inch pie.

The terms chess and cheese were apparently once used interchangeably in Britain; at least we know that a chessel or a chesset was a cheese vat. There has been debate and confusion over the difference, if any, between cheese pie and chess pie for many years. To this point, there is a reference in *Mrs. Porter's New Southern Cookery Book,* written by a Virginian in 1871. First, she gives a recipe for "Real Cheesecake." Never mind the cake part; it is a pie, baked in a pastry-lined tin. But it does call for "four ounces of rich (not strong or old) cheese," cut into small pieces and mixed with an equal weight of butter. This recipe is followed by five additional "cheesecakes," all of which are pies, not cakes, and none of which contains cheese. Today, we would refer to these as chess pies. In those days, if one wished to say "cheese," one was compelled to say, "real cheese." In this chapter we assume that cheesecakes and cheese pies contain cheese and that chess pies do not.

TYLER PUDDING PIE

¼ cup plus 2 tablespoons butter or margarine, softened
1½ cups firmly packed brown sugar
3 eggs
¼ cup plus 2 tablespoons whipping cream
2 teaspoons grated lemon rind
3 tablespoons lemon juice
½ teaspoon ground cinnamon
¼ teaspoon ground allspice
1 unbaked (9-inch) pastry shell
1 tablespoon cornmeal

Cream butter and sugar; add eggs, one at a time, beating well after each addition. Add whipping cream, lemon rind, juice, cinnamon, and allspice; beat well. Pour filling into pastry shell. Sprinkle cornmeal evenly over top of filling. Bake at 300° for 45 minutes. Cool pie before slicing. Yield: one 9-inch pie.

DAMSON CARAMEL PIE

5 eggs, beaten
2 cups firmly packed light brown sugar
1 cup butter or margarine, melted
1 cup Damson Plum preserves
1 unbaked (9-inch) pastry shell

Combine eggs, sugar, butter, and preserves in a medium mixing bowl; beat at medium speed of an electric mixer until smooth. Pour filling into pastry shell. Bake at 350° for 45 minutes or until a knife inserted in center comes out clean. Cool pie completely before serving. Yield: one 9-inch pie.

TELFAIR TRANSPARENT PIE

1 cup butter or margarine, melted
1 (16-ounce) package light brown sugar
5 eggs
2 unbaked (9-inch) pastry shells
Sweetened whipped cream (optional)

Combine butter and sugar, mixing well. Add eggs, one at a time, beating well after each addition. Pour filling into pastry shells. Bake at 350° for 40 minutes or until a knife inserted in center comes out clean. Cool to room temperature. Serve with whipped cream, if desired. Yield: two 9-inch pies.

JOHN TYLER

LEE FAMILY ORANGE PIE

3 eggs, divided
½ cup sugar
2 tablespoons all-purpose flour
1 tablespoon butter or margarine, melted
1 tablespoon grated orange rind
1 cup orange juice
1 unbaked (9-inch) pastry shell
¼ cup plus 2 tablespoons sugar
Orange slices (optional)

Beat egg yolks until thick and lemon colored. Add ½ cup sugar, flour, butter, orange rind, and juice; mix well. Pour filling into pastry shell. Bake at 450° for 10 minutes. Reduce heat to 350°, and continue baking 25 minutes or until set.

Beat egg whites (at room temperature) until foamy. Gradually add ¼ cup plus 2 tablespoons sugar, 1 tablespoon at a time, beating until stiff peaks form. Spread meringue over hot filling, sealing to edge of pastry. Bake at 350° for 10 minutes or until golden brown. Chill. Garnish with orange slices, if desired. Yield: one 9-inch pie.

The Lee and Washington families were so intricately interrelated that their recipes, understandably, changed hands so often that sometimes the origins became vague. Our Lee Family Orange Pie was developed from a family manuscript recipe. In the laconic style of the day, the base recipe simply listed ingredients and ended with "bake." The directions are now complete and crystal clear.

NASHVILLE LEMON PIE

1 cup sugar
1 tablespoon all-purpose flour
4 eggs, beaten
1 cup light corn syrup
1 tablespoon grated lemon rind
3 tablespoons lemon juice
1 tablespoon plus 1 teaspoon butter or margarine, melted
1 unbaked (9-inch) pastry shell
Whipped cream (optional)
Grated lemon rind (optional)

Combine sugar and flour in a medium mixing bowl; add eggs, syrup, 1 tablespoon lemon rind, juice, and butter, mixing well.

Pour filling into pastry shell. Bake at 375° for 10 minutes. Reduce temperature to 350°; bake 45 minutes. Cool to room temperature. Garnish with whipped cream and sprinkle with lemon rind before serving, if desired. Yield: one 9-inch pie.

Robert E. Lee in His Study, *by A. J. Volck, 1870.*

OZARK SORGHUM-MOLASSES PIE

1 cup sugar
2 tablespoons all-purpose flour
½ cup sorghum
½ cup molasses
3 eggs, beaten
1 tablespoon butter or margarine, melted
1 tablespoon lemon juice
¾ cup chopped pecans (optional)
1 unbaked (9-inch) pastry shell
Ground nutmeg

Combine sugar, flour, sorghum, molasses, eggs, butter, and lemon juice in a large mixing bowl; beat well. Stir in pecans, if desired. Pour filling into pastry shell; sprinkle with nutmeg. Bake at 350° for 1 hour. Cool before slicing. Yield: one 9-inch pie.

OSGOOD PIE

4 eggs, separated
2 cups sugar
2 tablespoons vinegar
1 teaspoon ground ginger
1 teaspoon ground allspice
1 teaspoon ground cinnamon
1 teaspoon ground cloves
1 cup raisins
1 unbaked (9-inch) pastry shell

Beat egg yolks with a wire whisk in a large mixing bowl; add sugar, vinegar, spices, and raisins; mix well.
Beat egg whites (at room temperature) until stiff peaks form. Fold into raisin mixture. Pour filling into pastry shell. Bake at 375° for 45 to 50 minutes. Cool. Yield: one 9-inch pie.

Plesy Jones, center, operated a sorghum mill near the Yellow River in Gwinnett County, Georgia, in 1912.

JAMES K. POLK'S VINEGAR PIE

2 cups sugar
4 eggs, beaten
¼ cup butter or margarine, melted
¼ teaspoon salt
1 tablespoon apple cider vinegar
1 unbaked (9-inch) pastry shell

Combine first 5 ingredients in a medium mixing bowl, beating until well blended. Pour filling into pastry shell. Bake at 350° for 35 minutes. Cool before slicing. Yield: one 9-inch pie.

CHEESE PIES AND CHEESECAKES

"THE ORIGINAL" OLD-FASHIONED CHEESECAKE

1 (6-ounce) package
  zwieback toast,
  crushed
1 cup sugar
1 teaspoon ground
  cinnamon
½ cup butter or margarine,
  melted
4 cups small-curd cottage
  cheese
1 (8-ounce) package cream
  cheese, softened
1 (16-ounce) carton
  commercial sour cream
1½ cups sugar
¼ cup plus 2 tablespoons
  all-purpose flour
6 eggs, beaten
Grated rind and juice of
  1 lemon
1 teaspoon vanilla
  extract
Dash of salt

Combine toast crumbs, 1 cup sugar, cinnamon, and butter; mix well. Firmly press mixture

Cheese presses came in several shapes. This round, flat one was used for soft, fresh curd cheese; note drain holes for whey.

into bottom and sides of a 9-inch springform pan; set aside.

Place half of cottage cheese in container of an electric blender; blend until smooth, turning blender off every 15 seconds to scrape sides with a rubber spatula. Repeat procedure with remaining cottage cheese.

Combine cottage cheese and cream cheese in a large mixing bowl; beat at medium speed of electric mixer until light and fluffy. Add remaining ingredients, beating until fluffy.

Pour mixture into prepared crust. Bake at 325° for 1 hour. Turn oven off. Leaving oven door closed, allow cheesecake to remain in oven 1 hour. Remove from oven, and let cool to room temperature. Loosely cover, and refrigerate overnight. Remove sides of springform pan before serving. Yield: 16 to 20 servings.

Alternate Method: To prepare cheesecake using a food processor, position knife blade in food processor bowl; add cottage cheese. Process 3 to 5 seconds. Stop processor, and scrape sides of bowl with a rubber spatula. Process 3 to 5 additional seconds or until cottage cheese is smooth and creamy. Add cream cheese; repeat processing procedure until mixture is smooth and creamy.

KLEEMAN'S COTTAGE CHEESE PIE

1¼ cups cottage cheese
4 eggs
1¼ cups sugar
2 tablespoons all-purpose
  flour
¼ cup commercial sour
  cream
¼ cup butter or margarine,
  melted
2 teaspoons grated lemon
  rind
¼ cup lemon juice
1 unbaked (9-inch) pastry
  shell
Orange slices (optional)

Place cottage cheese in container of an electric blender; process until smooth. Set aside.

Beat eggs in a medium mixing bowl until thick and lemon colored; add sugar and flour, beating until well blended. Add cottage cheese, sour cream, butter, lemon rind and juice; beat until smooth.

Pour cheese mixture into pastry shell. Bake at 350° for 45 minutes or until a knife inserted in center comes out clean. Garnish with orange slices, if desired. Serve cheese pie warm or chilled. Yield: one 9-inch pie.

Kleeman's Cottage Cheese Pie (front) and Mocha Cheesecake.

MOCHA CHEESECAKE

2 cups graham cracker
　crumbs
½ cup butter or margarine,
　melted
2 tablespoons sugar
1 (8-ounce) package
　semisweet chocolate
　squares
1 (8-ounce) carton
　commercial sour cream,
　divided
3 (8-ounce) packages cream
　cheese, softened
1 cup sugar
2 eggs
½ cup cold strong coffee
1 teaspoon vanilla extract
Whipped cream (optional)

Combine first 3 ingredients; mix well. Firmly press mixture into bottom of a 10-inch spring-form pan.

Place chocolate squares in top of a double boiler; place over boiling water. Reduce heat to low; cook until chocolate melts. Remove from heat; stir in 2 ta-blespoons sour cream. Set mix-ture aside to cool.

Beat cream cheese at medium speed of an electric mixer until light and fluffy; gradually add 1 cup sugar, mixing well. Add eggs, one at a time, beating well after each addition. Add choco-late, remaining sour cream, cof-fee, and vanilla; mix well.

Pour mixture into prepared pan. Bake at 350° for 45 min-utes. (Filling will become firm as pie stands.) Let cool to room temperature on a wire rack; chill 8 hours or overnight.

To serve, remove sides of springform pan. Garnish with whipped cream, if desired. Yield: 10 to 12 servings.

Alternate Method: To prepare cheesecake filling using a food processor, position knife blade in food processor bowl; add cream cheese, sugar, and eggs. Process 2 minutes. Stop proces-sor, and scrape sides of bowl with a rubber spatula. Process 1 to 2 additional minutes or until mixture is smooth. Add cooled chocolate mixture, sour cream, coffee, and vanilla; mix well and proceed with recipe.

G reek author Athenæus compiled a cooking anthology fifteen volumes long in 228 A.D. Researching litera-ture up to 500 years old, he found that what every man hungered for was cheesecake. Poets praised it; philoso-phers argued the merits of different recipes. Wealthy, status-seeking Romans employed Greek chefs; cheesecake began the journey so many foods had taken, throughout Europe and the Roman Empire. It picked up the flavors and accents of each culture it touched, including American: Cream cheese was invented in New York in 1872.

JENNIE SELLIGMAN'S CREAM CHEESECAKE

1 (6-ounce) package zwieback
   toast, crushed
1 cup sugar
¾ teaspoon ground cinnamon
¼ cup plus 2 tablespoons
   butter or margarine, melted
1 (8-ounce) package cream
   cheese, softened
¾ cup sugar
2 tablespoons all-purpose
   flour
4 eggs, separated
1 (16-ounce) carton
   commercial sour cream
1 teaspoon grated lemon rind
1½ tablespoons lemon juice
¾ teaspoon vanilla extract

Combine toast crumbs, 1 cup sugar, cinnamon, and butter, mixing well. Firmly press mixture into bottom and halfway up sides of a 9-inch springform pan; set aside.

Beat cream cheese at medium speed of an electric mixer until light and fluffy; gradually add ¾ cup sugar and flour, mixing well. Add egg yolks, sour cream, lemon rind, juice, and vanilla; mix well.

Beat egg whites (at room temperature) until stiff peaks form. Fold egg whites into cream cheese mixture.

Pour cheese mixture into crust. Bake at 375° for 5 minutes. Reduce heat to 300°; bake one hour and 10 minutes. Let cool to room temperature. Loosely cover, and refrigerate overnight. Remove sides of springform pan before serving. Yield: 12 to 16 servings.

Frontispiece of 1917 cookbook titled Simple Directions for the Cook.

Jennie Selligman was a Louisville hostess renowned for her food. While living in a downtown hotel, she once gave her personal cottage cheese cake recipe to the chef, asking him to prepare it for a party she was giving. While the chef was going about his work, a representative from a cheese manufacturer came into the kitchen to watch. He asked Mrs. Selligman if he might take her recipe back to the company laboratory and try it out with his product. With her permission, he did so. Mrs. Selligman, obviously pleased with the result, gave the recipe, now made with cream cheese, to Marion Flexner for her 1949 book, *Out of Kentucky Kitchens.*

The Cliff Owen dairy, near Winchester, Kentucky, c.1905.

GERMAN CHEESECAKE

1 cup all-purpose flour
2 tablespoons sugar
¼ teaspoon salt
¼ cup butter or margarine, softened
1 egg, beaten
2 (8-ounce) packages cream cheese, softened
1 (16-ounce) carton commercial sour cream
3 eggs, separated
2 teaspoons vanilla extract
¾ teaspoon lemon rind
3 tablespoons cornstarch
1 cup sugar

Combine first 3 ingredients in a mixing bowl; make a well in center of mixture. Add butter and egg; stir with a fork until dry ingredients are moistened. Shape dough into a ball; chill at least 2 hours.

Grease and flour bottom of a 9-inch springform pan. Roll pastry to ⅛-inch thickness on a lightly floured surface. Cut into a 9-inch circle. Place in bottom of springform pan. Bake at 450° for 10 minutes; cool.

Beat cream cheese in a large mixing bowl at medium speed of an electric mixer until smooth. Add sour cream, mixing well. Gradually add egg yolks, vanilla, lemon rind, cornstarch, and 1 cup sugar, mixing well.

Beat egg whites (at room temperature) until stiff peaks form. Gently fold into cream cheese mixture.

Pour mixture into prepared pan. Bake at 350° for 45 minutes. Increase temperature to 375°; continue baking 15 minutes. Turn oven off. Leaving oven door closed, allow cheesecake to cool in oven for 1 hour. Remove from oven; let cool to room temperature. Loosely cover and refrigerate 12 to 24 hours. (Cheesecake is best when thoroughly chilled and flavors have time to ripen.) Remove sides of springform pan before serving. Yield: about 12 servings.

Illustration from Sunkist Orange Recipes *booklet, 1940.*

PINEAPPLE-COTTAGE CHEESE PIE

1 cup cream-style cottage cheese
4 eggs, separated
1⅓ cups sugar
1 cup whipping cream
2 (15¼-ounce) cans crushed pineapple, drained and divided
1 unbaked (10-inch) pastry shell
¼ teaspoon cream of tartar
Pinch of salt
¼ cup sugar

Place cottage cheese in container of an electric blender; process 15 to 20 seconds or until smooth. Set aside.

Beat egg yolks until thick and lemon colored. Gradually add sugar, beating well. Add cottage cheese, whipping cream, and half of pineapple; mix until thoroughly blended.

Beat 2 egg whites (at room temperature) until stiff peaks form. Fold into pineapple-cheese mixture.

Spread remaining pineapple over bottom of pastry shell. Gently spoon pineapple-cheese filling over pineapple layer. Bake at 350° for 50 minutes.

Combine remaining 2 egg whites (at room temperature), cream of tartar, and salt; beat until foamy. Gradually add ¼ cup sugar, 1 tablespoon at a time, beating until stiff peaks form and sugar dissolves. Spread meringue over hot filling, sealing to edge of pastry. Bake at 350° for 10 minutes or until meringue is lightly browned. Cool before slicing. Yield: one 10-inch pie.

BLUE RIBBON ORANGE CHEESECAKE

1½ cups graham cracker crumbs
3 tablespoons sugar
½ cup butter or margarine, melted
3 (8-ounce) packages cream cheese, softened
1 cup sugar
3 eggs
½ cup butter or margarine, melted
½ teaspoon orange extract
Whipped cream (optional)
Grated orange rind (optional)

Combine first 3 ingredients in a medium mixing bowl; mix well. Firmly press mixture into bottom and about ¾ inch up the sides of a 9-inch springform pan; set aside.

Beat cream cheese with an electric mixer until light and fluffy. Gradually add 1 cup sugar, mixing well. Add eggs, one at a time, beating well after each addition. Stir in remaining ½ cup butter and orange extract; mix well.

Pour mixture into pan. Bake at 450° for 15 minutes. (Filling will become firm as the cake stands.) Cool to room temperature on a wire rack; refrigerate at least 12 hours.

Remove sides of springform pan. Garnish cheesecake with whipped cream and orange rind, if desired. Yield: 10 to 12 servings.

PINEAPPLE CHEESECAKE

1½ cups graham cracker crumbs
⅔ cup sugar
½ cup butter or margarine, melted
2 (8-ounce) packages cream cheese, softened
½ cup sugar
2 tablespoons all-purpose flour
3 eggs
1 (8¼-ounce) can crushed pineapple, well-drained
2 teaspoons vanilla extract, divided
1 (8-ounce) carton commercial sour cream
3 tablespoons sugar

Combine first 3 ingredients in a mixing bowl; mix well. Press into bottom and halfway up sides of a 9-inch springform pan; set aside.

Beat cream cheese at medium speed of an electric mixer until light and fluffy. Gradually add ½ cup sugar and flour, beating well. Add eggs, one at a time, beating well after each addition. Stir in pineapple and 1 teaspoon vanilla. Pour into prepared pan. Bake at 375° for 20 minutes. Remove from oven; cool 15 minutes.

Combine sour cream, 3 tablespoons sugar, and remaining vanilla, mixing well; spread over cheesecake. Bake at 425° for 10 minutes. Remove from oven, and let cool 30 minutes. Remove sides from springform pan. Cool completely. Cover cheesecake loosely, and refrigerate overnight. Yield: 12 to 16 servings.

Heady stuff, this: The anonymous designer of the Proteus Float, "Ceres," for the 1886 Mardi Gras inspired an anonymous writer to an effusive description of Ceres as "A planet where fruits abound. A luscious land is this. . . . Towering above them all, the King of Fruits, is the Pine-Apple, yellow and mellow, and glorious and somewhat disdainful of his smaller and less noble brothers. . . . A fragrance far greater than mortal senses can enjoy or endure, fills the mental nostril as this vision is beheld."

The Proteus Float, entitled "Ceres," 1866 Mardi Gras.

Praline Cheesecake, one of the things to like about the South.

PRALINE CHEESECAKE

1¼ cups graham cracker crumbs
¼ cup sugar
¼ cup chopped pecans, toasted
¼ cup butter or margarine, melted
3 (8-ounce) packages cream cheese, softened
1 cup firmly packed light brown sugar
1 (5.33-ounce) can evaporated milk
2 tablespoons all-purpose flour
3 eggs
1½ teaspoons vanilla extract
1 cup pecan halves, toasted
Glaze (recipe follows)

Combine first 4 ingredients, mixing well. Press mixture into bottom and 1½ inches up the sides of a 9-inch springform pan. Bake at 350° for 5 minutes.

Beat cream cheese at medium speed of an electric mixer until light and fluffy. Gradually add sugar, milk, and flour, mixing well. Add eggs, one at a time, beating well after each addition. Stir in vanilla. Pour into prepared pan. Bake at 350° for 55 to 60 minutes.

Let cool in pan 30 minutes. Loosen and remove sides of springform pan; cool completely. Cover loosely, and refrigerate overnight.

Before serving, arrange pecan halves on top of cheesecake. Serve with warm glaze. Yield: 12 to 16 servings.

Glaze:

1 cup dark corn syrup
2 tablespoons firmly packed light brown sugar
1 tablespoon cornstarch
1 teaspoon vanilla extract

Combine first 3 ingredients in a small saucepan; bring to a boil. Reduce heat, and simmer 1 to 2 minutes, stirring occasionally. Remove from heat; cool slightly, and stir in vanilla. Serve glaze warm with cheesecake. Yield: 1 cup.

The recipes on these two pages probably represent the Americanization of cheesecake best of all. Where but in the South do we find the pecan and pumpkin growing with minimal help from man? Where but in America were graham crackers and cream cheese invented? Praline Cheesecake with chopped pecans in the crust and pecan halves on top and Pumpkin Cheesecake garnished with pecans — just try ordering either of these Southern specialties in a European restaurant! Perhaps the best way to enjoy these is to make them.

PUMPKIN CHEESECAKE

¼ cup butter or margarine, softened
1 cup plus 1⅓ tablespoons sugar, divided
1 egg
1¼ cups all-purpose flour
2 (8-ounce) packages cream cheese, softened
2 eggs
2 cups cooked, mashed pumpkin
1 teaspoon ground cinnamon
¼ teaspoon ground ginger
¼ teaspoon ground nutmeg
⅛ teaspoon salt
Whipped cream
Toasted pecans

Corn shocks and pumpkins stand warm in the sunshine of a Virginia field.

Cream butter; gradually add ⅓ cup sugar and 1 egg, beating well. Gradually add flour, stirring until well blended. Firmly press mixture into bottom and halfway up sides of a 9-inch springform pan. Set aside.

Beat cream cheese at medium speed of an electric mixer until smooth; gradually add remaining sugar, beating well. Add 2 eggs, one at a time, beating well after each addition.

Combine pumpkin, spices, and salt; stir well, and add to cream cheese mixture. Mix well. Pour mixture into prepared pan. Bake at 350° for 50 minutes. Remove from oven, and let cool to room temperature; chill overnight. Remove sides from springform pan.

Pipe whipped cream in a decorative design around base and on top of cake. Garnish with pecans. Yield: 8 to 10 servings.

PRIDE
OF THE COOK

Cream Pies, Plain and Fancy

The cream pies in this chapter are those whose fillings are cooked and then poured into a baked, or otherwise prepared, pie shell. We lead off with basic ones, smooth and creamy, and progress to those with distinctive additions. Baked pastry shells are required for some, crumb or crisp meringue crusts for others. Graham cracker crust, for example, is delicious with vanilla cream filling; years ago the recipe was on the cracker box, and it was the first pie some cooks ever learned to make. Crumb or meringue crusts are great for emergencies, needing only to be filled with ice cream.

Nearly every old cookbook published in the South had a pie named for Jefferson Davis (1808-1889), the Kentucky-born, West Point-educated President of the Confederacy. Although imprisoned for two years after the war, he received a pardon, and his birthday, June 3, is now a holiday in parts of the South. Opinions about the man varied widely as did the recipes for his namesake pie: Some versions, ours included, contain several spices, others only nutmeg.

If time and usage are measures of quality, as we believe, the Butterscotch Meringue Pie served for over fifty years at Smith and Welton's Tea Room in Norfolk, Virginia, will go to the head of the class. Alongside it goes the outstanding old-timer, Caramel Cream Pie, made the only true way, by melting part of the sugar.

Of the cream pies with additions, banana and coconut could tie for first place, with nut and fruit versions not far behind. Old Talbott Inn at Bardstown, Kentucky, has been serving Orange Meringue Pie for longer than anyone can remember. And the terrace and dining rooms of Allison's Little Tea House, Arlington, Virginia, have been known for Coconut Cream Pie since the 1920s. There's even a pie with a personal history: An Alabama woman long ago grew her own Ponderosa lemon tree, shielding it from the weather, in order to make her favorite Lemon Meringue Pie.

There is many a proud cream pie in this collection dating back to the days when recipes were "whispered" from mother to daughter.

A few of the creamiest cream pies the South has to offer (front to rear): Festive Cream Pie (page 101), Chocolate Cream Pie (page 92), and Lemon Meringue Pie (page 98). Flaky pastry underlies them all.

BASIC CREAM PIES

BUTTERMILK CREAM PIE

1 cup sugar
2 tablespoons all-purpose flour
2 cups buttermilk
2 eggs, separated
1 tablespoon lemon juice
1 baked (9-inch) pastry shell

Combine sugar, flour, buttermilk, egg yolks, and lemon juice in top of a double boiler. Cook mixture over boiling water, stirring constantly, 30 minutes or until thickened and smooth. Remove from heat. Pour filling into pastry shell.

Beat egg whites (at room temperature) until stiff peaks form. Spread over filling, sealing to edge of pastry. Bake at 425° for 8 minutes or until lightly browned. Cool. Refrigerate until chilled. Yield: one 9-inch pie.

VANILLA CREAM PIE

1 cup sugar
⅓ cup plus 2 tablespoons all-purpose flour
¼ teaspoon salt
2⅔ cups milk
4 eggs, beaten
2 tablespoons butter or margarine
½ teaspoon vanilla extract
1 baked (9-inch) chocolate wafer piecrust
Whole fresh raspberries
Whipped cream

Combine sugar, flour, and salt in a medium saucepan; add milk, stirring until smooth. Cook over medium heat, stirring constantly, until thickened and bubbly.

Gradually stir one-fourth of hot mixture into eggs; add to remaining hot mixture, stirring constantly. Cook, stirring constantly, 2 minutes or until mixture thickens. Remove from heat, and gently stir in butter and vanilla. Pour into chocolate wafer piecrust. Chill completely.

Garnish with fresh raspberries and whipped cream. Yield: one 9-inch pie.

Note: Fresh blueberries, kiwi, pineapple, or strawberries may be substituted for raspberries.

Vanilla Cream Pie, a basic recipe to flavor and garnish to taste.

VIRGINIA HOLIDAY CREAM PIE

Pastry for 1 double-crust
  (9-inch) pie
¾ cup sugar
¼ cup plus 1 tablespoon
  all-purpose flour
¼ teaspoon salt
2 cups milk
3 egg yolks
1 egg
1 teaspoon vanilla extract
1 cup whipping cream
2 tablespoons sugar
¼ teaspoon vanilla
  extract
Chopped red and
  green maraschino
  cherries
Chopped pecans

Roll half of pastry to ⅛-inch thickness on a lightly floured surface, and fit into a 9-inch pieplate. Trim excess pastry around edges. Fold edges under, and flute. Prick bottom and sides of shell with a fork.

Roll remaining half of pastry into an 8-inch circle, and place on a baking sheet. Bake pastry shell and pastry circle at 425° for 12 to 15 minutes or until golden brown. Cool.

Combine ¾ cup sugar, flour, and salt in top of a double boiler; stir in milk, egg yolks, and egg, mixing well. Cook over boiling water, stirring constantly, 20 minutes or until very thick and smooth. Remove from heat, and add 1 teaspoon vanilla. Let cool.

Beat whipping cream in a small mixing bowl until foamy; gradually add 2 tablespoons sugar, 1 tablespoon at a time, beating until soft peaks form. Stir in ¼ teaspoon vanilla.

Fold one-fourth whipped cream into custard mixture. Pour half of custard into baked pastry shell. Top with baked pastry circle and remaining custard. Cover with remaining whipped cream. Garnish with chopped maraschino cherries and pecans. Cool completely. Yield: one 9-inch pie.

Note: For a more festive pie, arrange cherries in the shape of a Christmas tree on top of pie.

Jefferson Davis passes through LaGrange, Georgia, April, 1886.

JEFF DAVIS PIE

1 cup sugar
3 tablespoons all-purpose
  flour
3 eggs, separated
1 cup whipping cream
1 cup milk
2 tablespoons butter or
  margarine
1 teaspoon vanilla extract
1 teaspoon ground cinnamon
¼ teaspoon ground nutmeg
⅛ teaspoon ground cloves
1 baked (9-inch) pastry shell
¼ teaspoon cream of tartar
¼ cup plus 2 tablespoons
  sugar

Combine 1 cup sugar and flour in top of a double boiler; mix well.

Combine egg yolks, whipping cream, and milk; beat well. Gradually stir into sugar mixture, mixing well. Cook over boiling water, stirring constantly, 20 minutes or until thickened. Remove from heat. Stir in butter, vanilla, and spices. Pour filling into pastry shell.

Beat egg whites (at room temperature) and cream of tartar until foamy. Gradually add ¼ cup plus 2 tablespoons sugar, 1 tablespoon at a time, beating until stiff peaks form. Spread meringue over filling, sealing to edge of pastry. Bake at 425° for 6 minutes or until meringue is lightly browned. Cool. Yield: one 9-inch pie.

Two versions of the origin of the controversial Jeff Davis pie recipe come close enough to agreeing that the background may be close enough to the truth to bear repeating: One George B. Warren moved from the South to Missouri just before the outbreak of the War Between the States, taking his cook Mary Ann (or Jule Ann) with him. She served a pie so heavenly tasting that, when asked the name, she said it was a Jeff Davis pie, out of loyalty to Mr. Warren, a Southern sympathizer.

Moonshine Pie, in this case made with bourbon.

SMITH AND WELTON'S TEA ROOM BUTTERSCOTCH MERINGUE PIE

1 cup firmly packed light
   brown sugar
¼ cup cornstarch
4 eggs, separated
2 cups milk
½ cup butter or margarine
1 teaspoon vanilla extract
1 baked (9-inch) pastry shell
Pinch of cream of tartar
¼ cup sugar

Combine brown sugar and cornstarch in top of a double boiler; mix well. Add egg yolks, milk, and butter, mixing well. Cook over boiling water, stirring constantly, 30 minutes or until thickened. Remove from heat; stir in vanilla. Pour filling into pastry shell.

Beat egg whites (at room temperature) and cream of tartar until foamy. Gradually add ¼ cup sugar, 1 tablespoon at a time, beating until stiff peaks form. Spread meringue over filling, sealing to edge of pastry. Bake at 350° for 10 minutes or until meringue is golden brown. Cool. Yield: one 9-inch pie.

One of the South's most respected old-line department stores, Smith and Welton's, opened first in Portsmouth, Virginia, in 1890. Around the turn of the century they moved to Granby Street in Norfolk. The store was managed by a member of the Welton family until recent years. Since 1933, when the Tea Room opened, there have been only three managers. Prices on the old menus may strike us as other-worldly: Soup at fifteen cents, pie ten cents! But at any price, the butterscotch pie here is a must.

MOONSHINE PIE

1 cup firmly packed light
   brown sugar, divided
¼ cup plus 1 tablespoon
   all-purpose flour
Dash of salt
1¼ cups milk
2 eggs, separated
2 tablespoons butter or
   margarine
1 tablespoon bourbon
1 (9-inch) coconut piecrust
Flaked coconut, toasted

Combine ¾ cup sugar, flour, and salt in top of a double boiler; add milk, stirring well. Cook over boiling water, stirring constantly, 20 minutes or until thickened.

Beat egg yolks until thick and lemon colored. Gradually stir about one-fourth hot mixture into yolks; add to remaining hot mixture. Cook 15 minutes over boiling water, stirring frequently. Remove from heat; stir in butter and bourbon. Cool.

Beat egg whites (at room temperature) until foamy; gradually add remaining ¼ cup sugar, 1 tablespoon at a time, beating until soft peaks form. Fold egg whites into custard mixture; spoon filling into coconut piecrust. Sprinkle with toasted coconut. Chill until set. Yield: one 9-inch pie.

OLD-FASHIONED CARAMEL CREAM PIE

2 cups sugar, divided
½ cup all-purpose flour
⅛ teaspoon salt
2 cups milk
4 egg yolks, beaten
1 baked (9-inch) pastry shell
Whipped cream

Combine 1 cup sugar, flour, and salt in a medium saucepan; add milk and egg yolks, stirring until smooth. Cook over medium heat, stirring constantly, until mixture is thickened and bubbly. Remove from heat, and set aside.

Sprinkle remaining sugar evenly in a 10-inch cast-iron skillet. Cook over medium heat, stirring constantly with a wooden spoon until sugar caramelizes. Remove from heat, and carefully pour into warm cream mixture. Stir until smooth.

Pour caramel mixture into pastry shell; chill completely. Serve with dollops of whipped cream. Yield: one 9-inch pie.

CHOCOLATE MERINGUE PIE

3 eggs, separated
¾ cup sugar
¼ cup plus 1 tablespoon all-purpose flour
2 (1-ounce) squares unsweetened chocolate, melted
¼ cup butter or margarine, melted
2 cups milk
2 teaspoons vanilla extract
Pinch of salt
1 baked (9-inch) pastry shell
¼ teaspoon cream of tartar
¼ cup plus 2 tablespoons sugar

Combine egg yolks, ¾ cup sugar, flour, chocolate, and butter in top of a double boiler; mix well. Gradually add milk, stirring well. Cook over boiling water, stirring constantly, 20 minutes or until thickened. Stir in vanilla and salt. Pour filling into pastry shell.

Beat egg whites (at room temperature) and cream of tartar until foamy. Gradually add ¼ cup plus 2 tablespoons sugar, 1 tablespoon at a time, beating until stiff peaks form. Spread meringue over filling, sealing to edge of pastry. Bake at 425° for 6 minutes or until meringue is lightly browned. Cool. Yield: one 9-inch pie.

Raymond Community Council women grading and packing the first case of eggs marketed by the cooperative in Coweta County, Georgia, in 1921.

Cocoa plantation scene used on advertising card, late 1800s.

CHOCOLATE CREAM PIE

1½ cups sugar
½ cup cocoa
½ cup all-purpose flour
3 eggs, beaten
1½ cups evaporated milk
1½ cups water
3 tablespoons butter or margarine
1½ teaspoons vanilla extract
1 baked (9-inch) pastry shell
1 cup whipping cream, whipped

Combine sugar, cocoa, and flour in a heavy saucepan; stir to remove lumps. Combine eggs, milk, and water in a mixing bowl. Gradually add milk mixture to cocoa mixture, stirring until well blended. Cook over medium heat, stirring constantly, until mixture thickens and comes to a boil. Cook 1 minute, stirring constantly. Remove from heat; add butter and vanilla, stirring until butter melts. Pour into pastry shell. Chill. Garnish with whipped cream. Yield: one 9-inch pie.

CHOCOLATE ANGEL PIE

Meringue Pie Shell
1 (4-ounce) package sweet baking chocolate
3 tablespoons water
2 egg yolks, beaten
1 cup whipping cream
1 tablespoon sifted powdered sugar
⅛ teaspoon ground cinnamon
Additional whipped cream
Chopped pecans

Prepare Meringue Pie Shell; set aside.

Combine chocolate and water in a heavy saucepan; cook over low heat until chocolate melts, stirring frequently. Remove from heat.

Gradually stir about one-fourth of chocolate mixture into egg yolks; add to remaining chocolate mixture, stirring constantly. Return to low heat; cook, stirring constantly, 1 minute or until smooth and thickened. Remove from heat; cool.

Beat 1 cup whipping cream until foamy; gradually add sugar and cinnamon, beating until soft peaks form. Spread 1 cup whipped cream mixture in bottom of meringue shell.

Gently fold chocolate mixture into remaining whipped cream mixture; spread over whipped cream layer. Chill at least 3 hours or overnight.

To serve, garnish with additional whipped cream and pecans. Yield: one 9-inch pie.

Meringue Pie Shell:

2 egg whites
⅛ teaspoon cream of tartar
⅛ teaspoon salt
½ cup sugar
½ cup chopped pecans
½ teaspoon vanilla extract

Beat egg whites (at room temperature), cream of tartar, and salt until foamy. Gradually add sugar, 1 tablespoon at a time, beating until stiff peaks form. Fold in pecans and vanilla. Spread meringue over bottom and sides of a greased 9-inch pieplate to form a pie shell. Bake at 275° for 50 to 55 minutes. Cool. Yield: one 9-inch pie shell.

FRUIT AND NUT CREAM PIES

KENTUCKY BANANA CREAM PIE

⅓ cup cornstarch
⅔ cup sugar
¼ teaspoon salt
3 cups milk, scalded
3 eggs, separated
2 tablespoons butter or margarine, melted
1 teaspoon vanilla extract
1 large banana, peeled and sliced
1 baked (9-inch) pastry shell
2 tablespoons sugar

Combine cornstarch, ⅔ cup sugar, and salt in top of a double boiler; mix well. Gradually add milk; cook over medium heat, stirring constantly, just until thickened.

Beat egg yolks until thick and lemon colored. Stir one-fourth hot mixture into yolks; add to remaining hot mixture, stirring constantly. Cook an additional 2 minutes or until thickened and bubbly. Remove from heat; stir in butter and vanilla.

Place banana slices in pastry shell. Pour filling over top.

Beat egg whites (at room temperature) until soft peaks form; gradually add 2 tablespoons sugar, and continue beating until stiff peaks form. Spread meringue over filling, sealing to edge of pastry. Bake at 350° for 5 minutes or until meringue is golden brown. Serve pie warm or chilled. Yield: one 9-inch pie.

COFFEE-ALMOND CREAM PIE

1 baked (9-inch) pastry shell
1 (2½-ounce) package sliced almonds, toasted and crumbled
¼ cup plus 1 tablespoon all-purpose flour
1 cup whipping cream, divided
1 egg, beaten
1 cup strong coffee
¾ cup sugar
⅛ teaspoon salt
1 teaspoon vanilla extract
Toasted sliced almonds (optional)
Whipped cream (optional)

Line bottom of pastry shell with almonds; set aside.

Combine flour, ¼ cup whipping cream, and egg in a small mixing bowl. Stir until smooth, and set aside.

Combine remaining ¾ cup whipping cream, coffee, sugar, and salt in top of a double boiler; place over boiling water. Cook, stirring constantly, until mixture is thoroughly heated.

Add reserved flour mixture to hot coffee mixture, stirring constantly, until smooth. Continue cooking until mixture becomes thickened and bubbly. Remove from heat, and stir in vanilla. Pour mixture into pastry shell. Chill thoroughly. Garnish pie with toasted sliced almonds and whipped cream, if desired. Yield: one 9-inch pie.

Label from Lord Calvert coffee, a mocha-java blend, c.1898.

ALLISON'S LITTLE TEA HOUSE COCONUT CREAM PIE

¼ cup all-purpose flour
2½ tablespoons cornstarch
1 egg
1 egg yolk
1¾ cups milk, divided
¾ cup sugar, divided
¼ teaspoon salt
1 tablespoon butter or
    margarine
½ teaspoon vanilla extract
2 egg whites
1 baked (9-inch) pastry shell
2 cups grated fresh coconut,
    divided

Combine flour, cornstarch, egg, egg yolk, and ½ cup milk in a small mixing bowl; stir until smooth. Set aside.

Combine remaining milk, ½ cup sugar, and salt in a medium saucepan. Cook over medium heat, stirring constantly, until mixture begins to boil. Slowly add reserved flour mixture, stirring constantly. Continue cooking, stirring constantly, until mixture is thickened and bubbly. Remove from heat; add butter and vanilla. Stir until butter melts. Set aside.

Beat egg whites (at room temperature) until foamy. Gradually add remaining ¼ cup sugar, 1 tablespoon at a time, beating until stiff peaks form. Gently fold egg whites into custard, blending well. Spoon mixture into pastry shell. Sprinkle top of pie with 1½ cups coconut. Toast remaining coconut and sprinkle over top. Chill thoroughly before serving. Yield: one 9-inch pie.

COCONUT-CHERRY CREAM PIE

3 eggs, separated
1 cup sugar, divided
¼ cup plus 1 tablespoon
    all-purpose flour
½ teaspoon salt
2 cups milk
1 cup flaked coconut,
    divided
1½ teaspoons vanilla
    extract, divided
1 (16-ounce) can tart
    cherries, drained
1 baked (9-inch) pastry
    shell
2 tablespoons water

Beat egg yolks until well blended; set aside. Combine ½ cup sugar, flour, and salt in top of a double boiler; stir in milk and egg yolks. Cook over boiling water, stirring constantly, 10 minutes or until mixture is very thick and smooth. Remove from heat; stir in ½ cup coconut and 1 teaspoon vanilla. Set aside.

Arrange half of cherries in a layer in pastry shell. Pour coconut mixture over cherries. Set aside.

Beat egg whites (at room temperature) in top of a double boiler until foamy. Add remaining ½ cup sugar and 2 tablespoons water. Place over boiling water. Beat at high speed of an electric mixer until stiff peaks form. Remove from heat; add remaining ½ teaspoon vanilla. Beat until well blended. Spread meringue over filling, sealing to edge of pastry.

Arrange remaining cherries on top of meringue, and sprinkle with remaining coconut. Bake at 350° for 12 minutes or until meringue is golden brown. Cool to room temperature; chill. Yield: one 9-inch pie.

Note: Two cups of any fruit may be substituted for cherries.

*Allison's Little Tea
House Coconut Cream
Pie: Fresh coconut
is the secret.*

Could this be Bernhardt doing "Camille" under coconut palms? Late 1800s advertising card.

COCONUT-PINEAPPLE CREAM PIE

¾ cup sugar
¼ cup plus 1 tablespoon all-purpose flour
¼ teaspoon salt
2 cups milk
3 eggs, separated
1 cup flaked coconut, divided
2 teaspoons vanilla extract
1 (8-ounce) can pineapple tidbits, well-drained
1 baked (9-inch) pastry shell
¾ cup sugar
Dash of salt
3 tablespoons water
½ teaspoon vanilla extract

Combine ¾ cup sugar, flour, and ¼ teaspoon salt in top of a double boiler; stir in milk and egg yolks, mixing well. Cook over boiling water, stirring constantly, 20 minutes or until very thick and smooth. Remove from heat. Stir in ½ cup coconut and 2 teaspoons vanilla.

Place half of pineapple tidbits in pastry shell. Pour filling over pineapple.

Beat reserved egg whites (at room temperature) in top of a double boiler until foamy. Add ¾ cup sugar, salt, and water. Place over boiling water. Beat at high speed of an electric mixer until soft peaks form. Remove from heat; add ½ teaspoon vanilla. Beat well. Spread meringue over filling, sealing to edge of pastry. Arrange remaining pineapple over meringue; sprinkle with remaining coconut. Serve immediately. Yield: one 9-inch pie.

COCONUT MERINGUE PIE

¾ cup sugar
3 tablespoons cornstarch
¼ teaspoon salt
5 eggs, separated
2½ cups milk
1¼ cups flaked coconut, divided
½ teaspoon vanilla extract
1 baked (9-inch) pastry shell
¾ cup sugar

Combine sugar, cornstarch, and salt in top of a double boiler. Beat egg yolks until thick and lemon colored; add to sugar mixture, mixing well. Add milk; cook over boiling water, stirring constantly, 20 minutes or until mixture is very thick and smooth.

Remove from heat; gently stir in 1 cup coconut and vanilla. Pour filling into pastry shell.

Beat egg whites (at room temperature) until foamy. Gradually add ¾ cup sugar, 1 tablespoon at a time, beating until stiff peaks form. Spread meringue over hot filling, sealing to edge of pastry. Sprinkle with remaining coconut. Bake at 375° for 15 minutes or until meringue is golden brown. Cool to room temperature; chill. Yield: one 9-inch pie.

FRESH COCONUT CREAM PIE

1 cup sugar
⅔ cup cornstarch
¼ teaspoon salt
1 quart milk
4 egg yolks
2 tablespoons butter
1½ teaspoons vanilla
   extract
1 cup finely chopped fresh
   coconut, divided
1 baked (9-inch) pastry
   shell
½ cup whipping cream
1 teaspoon powdered sugar

Combine sugar, cornstarch, and salt in a heavy saucepan; stir in milk. Cook over medium heat, stirring constantly, until thickened and smooth.

Beat egg yolks until thick and lemon colored. Gradually stir about one-fourth of hot milk mixture into yolks; add to remaining hot milk mixture, stirring constantly. Cook 5 minutes, stirring constantly. Remove from heat; add butter and vanilla. Cool. Stir ⅔ cup coconut into cooled filling. Pour filling into pastry shell; chill overnight.

Beat whipping cream until foamy; gradually add powdered sugar, beating until soft peaks form. Spread over pie; sprinkle with remaining coconut. Yield: one 9-inch pie.

CRUNCHY PEANUT CREAM PIE

½ cup sugar
½ cup all-purpose flour
Pinch of salt
2¼ cups milk
3 eggs, separated
1 teaspoon vanilla
½ cup powdered sugar,
   sifted
⅓ cup crunchy peanut
   butter
1 baked (9-inch) pastry shell
¼ cup plus 2 tablespoons
   sugar

Combine sugar, flour, and salt in a heavy saucepan. Mix well to remove lumps. Gradually add milk, stirring until well blended. Bring to a boil; reduce heat, and cook, stirring constantly, until smooth and thickened. Remove from heat.

Beat egg yolks until thick and lemon colored. Gradually stir about half of hot mixture into yolks; add to remaining hot mixture, stirring constantly. Cook over low heat 2 minutes, stirring constantly. Remove from heat; stir in vanilla. Cool to room temperature.

Place powdered sugar and peanut butter in a mixing bowl; cut in peanut butter with a pastry blender until mixture is crumbly.

Place half of peanut butter mixture in pastry shell. Pour cooled filling over mixture; top with remaining peanut butter mixture.

Beat egg whites (at room temperature) until foamy. Gradually add ¼ cup plus 2 tablespoons sugar, 1 tablespoon at a time, beating until stiff peaks form and sugar dissolves. Spread meringue over filling, sealing to edge of pastry. Bake at 375° for 8 minutes or until meringue is lightly browned. Cool to room temperature before serving. Yield: one 9-inch pie.

GRAPE JUICE PIE

¾ cup sugar
¼ cup cornstarch
1⅓ cups grape juice
1 egg, slightly beaten
2 tablespoons butter
2 tablespoons lemon juice
1 baked (9-inch) pastry
   shell
1 cup whipping cream
1 tablespoon sugar

Combine sugar and cornstarch in a 2-quart saucepan. Stir in grape juice; cook over medium heat, stirring constantly, until thickened and bubbly. Cook 1 minute.

Add a small amount of hot mixture to egg, mixing well; stir egg mixture into remaining hot mixture. Add butter and lemon juice; return to heat. Bring to a boil, stirring constantly; boil gently 1 minute. Cool. Pour into pastry shell; chill thoroughly.

Combine whipping cream and sugar, beating until light and fluffy. Spread on pie; chill. Yield: 8 servings.

HEAVENLY LEMON PIE

4 eggs, separated
¼ teaspoon cream of tartar
1½ cups sugar, divided
1 tablespoon grated lemon
   rind
3 tablespoons lemon juice
⅛ teaspoon salt
1 cup whipping cream,
   whipped
Additional whipped cream

Beat egg whites (at room temperature) until foamy; add cream of tartar, beating slightly. Gradually add 1 cup sugar, beating well after each addition; continue beating egg mixture until stiff and glossy. Do not underbeat mixture.

Spoon meringue into a well-greased 9-inch pieplate. Use a spoon to shape meringue into a pie shell, swirling sides high. Bake at 275° for 50 minutes. Set aside to cool.

Beat egg yolks until thick and lemon colored. Gradually add remaining ½ cup sugar, lemon rind and juice, and salt. Cook in top of a double boiler, stirring constantly, until smooth and thickened. Cool mixture.

Fold 1 cup whipped cream into lemon mixture; spoon into meringue shell, and spread evenly. Cover and refrigerate at least 12 hours. Top with additional whipped cream. Yield: one 9-inch pie.

Buster Keaton, pie in hand, starred in the movie The Villain Still Pursued Her.

Alice Faye and Buster Keaton in the midst of a pie melée.

Back in the '30s and '40s, you plunked down a dime at the picture show, stopped by the popcorn machine, got a front seat, and prepared to howl. Buster Keaton, Harold Lloyd, Charlie Chaplin, the Marx Brothers; all made you — forced you to — laugh. In the hands of these comic masters, pie-throwing scenes reached the heights of hilarity, if not of art. Set-up: The "good" guy grabs the pie — the "bad" guy gets it in the face. Dénouement: A pie-throwing melée which broke the audience up. Folks were desperate for laughs.

FLORIDA LIME PIE

3 eggs, separated
1 cup sugar, divided
¼ cup lime juice
3 tablespoons hot
   water
Pinch of salt
1 baked (9-inch) graham
   cracker piecrust
Whipped cream
   (optional)
Lime slices (optional)

Beat egg yolks until thick and lemon colored in top of a double boiler. Add ½ cup sugar, lime juice, water, and salt; place over boiling water. Cook, stirring constantly, until thickened and smooth. Cool.

Beat egg whites (at room temperature) until foamy. Gradually add remaining ½ cup sugar, beating until stiff peaks form. Fold whites into lime mixture. Pour mixture into graham cracker piecrust. Bake at 325° for 10 minutes or until lightly browned. Chill at least 1 hour. Garnish with whipped cream and lime slices, if desired. Yield: one 9-inch pie.

LEMON MERINGUE PIE

1½ cups sugar
½ cup cornstarch
¼ teaspoon salt
1¾ cups water
4 eggs, separated
1 tablespoon butter or
   margarine, softened
2 tablespoons grated lemon
   rind
¼ cup fresh lemon juice
1 baked (9-inch) pastry shell
½ teaspoon cream of tartar
¼ cup plus 2 tablespoons
   sugar

Combine 1½ cups sugar, cornstarch, and salt in a medium saucepan. Gradually add water, stirring until well blended. Cook over medium heat, stirring constantly, until thickened.

Beat egg yolks until thick and lemon colored; gradually add one-fourth of hot mixture to yolks. Stir yolk mixture into remaining hot mixture. Cook over low heat 2 minutes.

Remove from heat. Add butter, lemon rind, and juice, stirring until butter melts. Pour filling into pastry shell.

Beat egg whites (at room temperature) and cream of tartar until foamy. Gradually add ¼ cup plus 2 tablespoons sugar. Beat until stiff peaks form. Spread over warm filling, sealing to edge of pastry. Bake at 350° for 12 to 15 minutes or until meringue is golden brown. Cool to room temperature. Yield: one 9-inch pie.

Old Talbott Tavern Orange Meringue Pie, an ambrosial combination.

OLD TALBOTT TAVERN ORANGE MERINGUE PIE

¾ cup sugar
½ cup all-purpose flour
¼ teaspoon salt
1¼ cups water
2 eggs, separated
2 teaspoons grated orange rind
½ cup orange juice
2 tablespoons lemon juice
1 baked (9-inch) pastry shell or graham cracker piecrust
½ cup sugar
Dash of salt
2 tablespoons water
1 orange, peeled, seeded, and separated into sections
½ cup flaked coconut

Combine ¾ cup sugar, flour, and ¼ teaspoon salt in top of a double boiler. Gradually add 1¼ cups water, stirring well. Place over boiling water, and cook, stirring constantly, until mixture thickens.

Beat egg yolks until thick and lemon colored. Gradually stir one-fourth of hot mixture into yolks; add to remaining hot mixture, stirring constantly. Cook over boiling water, stirring constantly, 5 minutes or until smooth and thickened.

Remove from heat. Stir in orange rind, orange juice, and lemon juice, mixing well. Spoon filling into pastry shell.

Combine egg whites, ½ cup sugar, dash of salt, and 2 tablespoons water in top of a double boiler; beat well. Place over boiling water. Beat at high speed of an electric mixer for 1 minute. Remove from heat; beat 1 minute or until soft peaks form. Spread meringue over filling, sealing to edge of pastry. Arrange orange sections over meringue; sprinkle with coconut. Chill. Yield: one 9-inch pie.

The Stone Inn, later renamed Old Talbott Tavern, was built in 1779 at Bardstown, Kentucky, in the path of the westward migration. It is the oldest western stagecoach stop in America. The thick stone walls and heavy timbers of the original building, as well as the old fireplaces, are still in place. A narrow stair led to a loft which was divided into two compartments, one for men and one for women. Statesmen and scoundrels alike passed the night and enjoyed the food here. Visitors to Kentucky still consider a visit to this charming inn a treat.

ORANGE MERINGUE PIE

1 cup sugar
¼ cup cornstarch
¼ teaspoon salt
1 cup orange juice
½ cup water
2 tablespoons lime juice
3 eggs, separated
Rind of 1 orange, grated
1 tablespoon butter or margarine
1 baked (9-inch) graham cracker piecrust
⅛ teaspoon cream of tartar
¼ cup plus 2 tablespoons sugar

Combine first 3 ingredients in top of a double boiler. Gradually add orange juice, water, lime juice, and egg yolks; stir until smooth. Cook over boiling water, stirring constantly, until thickened and smooth. Remove from heat; stir in orange rind and butter. Pour filling into graham cracker piecrust.

Beat egg whites (at room temperature) and cream of tartar until foamy. Gradually add remaining sugar, 1 tablespoon at a time, beating until stiff peaks form. Spread meringue over hot filling, sealing to edge of pastry. Bake at 350° for 10 minutes or until meringue is golden brown. Cool to room temperature before serving. Yield: one 9-inch pie.

"Oh, you naughty man," is first line spoken in this domestic melodrama. Next, "Sh . . . my wife's coming!" Then "What does this mean?" is a rhetorical question on the lips of the scandalized wife.

"Ma" Ferguson, 1933

Institute of Texan Cultures

MA FERGUSON'S PECAN CREAM PIE

1 cup sugar
½ cup chopped pecans
2 tablespoons all-purpose flour
2 eggs, separated
1 cup milk
2 tablespoons butter or margarine
2 teaspoons vanilla extract
1 baked (9-inch) pastry shell
¼ cup sugar
¼ teaspoon vanilla extract
2 tablespoons finely chopped pecans

Combine 1 cup sugar, ½ cup pecans, and flour in a heavy saucepan; stir well.

Combine egg yolks and milk in a mixing bowl; mix well.

Gradually add milk mixture to pecan mixture, stirring until well blended. Cook over medium heat, stirring constantly, until mixture thickens and comes to a boil. Cook 1 minute, stirring constantly. Remove from heat; add butter and 2 teaspoons vanilla, stirring until butter melts. Pour into pastry shell.

Beat egg whites (at room temperature) until foamy. Add ¼ cup sugar, 1 tablespoon at a time, beating until stiff peaks form. Beat in ¼ teaspoon vanilla. Spread meringue over filling; seal to edge of pastry. Sprinkle with pecans. Bake at 400° for 10 minutes or until golden brown. Cool. Yield: one 9-inch pie.

Miriam Amanda Wallace (1875-1961) was born into a family rich in Texas land and cattle. She married wealthy James Ferguson, who became governor of Texas in 1914. During his second term, he was convicted of irregularities and imprisoned. M. A. Ferguson (her name shortened to Ma by the press) was elected governor in 1924 and again in 1932. She pardoned her husband and hundreds of other prisoners. Reviews are mixed, but she left her mark on Texas politics.

PECAN-BUTTERSCOTCH PIE

½ cup firmly packed dark
    brown sugar
¼ cup cornstarch
¼ teaspoon salt
2 cups milk
¼ cup light corn syrup
3 eggs, separated
3 tablespoons butter or
    margarine
1 teaspoon vanilla extract
1 cup chopped pecans,
    divided
1 baked (9-inch) pastry shell
¼ teaspoon cream of tartar
Pinch of salt
¼ cup plus 2 tablespoons
    sugar

Combine brown sugar, cornstarch, and ¼ teaspoon salt in
top of a double boiler; add milk
and syrup, stirring well. Cook
over boiling water, stirring constantly, 20 minutes or until
thickened.

Beat egg yolks until thick and
lemon colored. Gradually stir
one-fourth of hot mixture into
yolks; add to remaining hot
mixture, stirring constantly.
Cook 5 minutes over boiling

water, stirring frequently. Remove from heat; stir in butter,
vanilla, and ¾ cup pecans. Pour
into pastry shell.

Beat egg whites (at room temperature), cream of tartar, and
pinch of salt until foamy. Gradually add sugar, 1 tablespoon at
a time, beating until stiff peaks
form. Spread meringue over filling, sealing to edge of pastry.
Sprinkle with remaining ¼ cup
pecans. Bake at 350° for 12 minutes or until meringue is golden
brown. Cool to room temperature. Chill thoroughly. Yield:
one 9-inch pie.

FESTIVE CREAM PIE

4 egg yolks, beaten
2⅓ cups whipping cream,
    divided
1 cup sugar
1 tablespoon all-purpose flour
½ cup finely chopped pecans
¼ cup finely chopped dates
¼ cup finely chopped candied
    cherries
¼ cup finely chopped raisins
1 baked (9-inch) pastry shell
2 tablespoons sugar
Additional finely chopped
    pecans

Combine egg yolks, 1⅓ cups
whipping cream, 1 cup sugar,
and flour in a heavy saucepan,
beating well. Cook over medium
heat, stirring constantly, until
thickened and bubbly. Stir in ½
cup pecans, dates, cherries, and
raisins; cook 2 to 3 minutes.
Pour into pastry shell. Cool.

Before serving, beat remaining 1 cup whipping cream until
foamy. Gradually add 2 tablespoons sugar, beating until soft
peaks form. Spread whipped
cream over filling, and sprinkle
with additional chopped
pecans. Yield: one 9-inch pie.

CHILL TO SET

Chiffon and Icebox Pies

A great many of our refrigerated pies are based on gelatin; we take them so for granted that it is odd to realize just how lately they've arrived. There is scarcely an account of an important ceremonial menu in Southern history that fails to mention "jellies" among the sweet offerings; hostesses depended upon those jellies to prettify a table. They were not Jell-O, not yet. They were calves' foot jelly, clarified, sweetened, flavored, and colored with such natural dyes as beetroot or spinach. Then came a gel that combined hartshorn with isinglass, a product made from the air bladders of fish, not (the other meaning) from thin sheets of mica! This concoction was unanimously considered a poor substitute for calves' foot jelly, and it was expensive as well.

Efforts at making commercial gelatin from bones were made in France in the late 1600s. Nobody paid much attention until the Revolution, when starvation was rampant. The French government accelerated a program to make gelatin into a nourishing diet product for the poor. It was put into the food in institutions and people ate it, although it is reputed to have tasted terrible. It was a start, however.

The plain granulated gelatin we use for so many of our refrigerated pies is still made from the bones of beef and veal, along with some connective tissue from the skin, but what is blissfully missing is the noisome flavor of the early gelatin. We simply open a packet, soften it in cold water, dissolve it in hot liquid, and rely on it to congeal a pint of liquid. Marion Harland used commercial "Coxe's Gelatin" in *Breakfast, Luncheon and Tea*, 1877. She even whipped cream into some dessert gels and jelled them in molds. Today, we fill a pie shell with a similar mixture and call it chiffon.

By the 1920s, gelatin as we know it had been introduced, and the time was right for the advent of the icebox pies. Not only were iron sinks and stoves becoming commonplace, modern homes were being built with iceboxes installed in kitchen walls so that ice could be put in from outside. Refrigerated pies, chiffon pies . . . they are old-hat delicacies to us, but they are our newest traditional pastry.

Cloud-light Pumpkin Chiffon Pie (page 111) reposes atop an antique icebox. On the shelf is French Silk Chocolate Pie (page 112), and on ice block is Tart Lemon Chiffon Pie (page 107).

CHIFFON PIES

BAVARIAN PIE

3 eggs, separated
½ cup sugar
¼ teaspoon salt
1 cup milk, scalded
1 envelope unflavored gelatin
¼ cup cold water
1 teaspoon vanilla extract
1 cup whipping cream, whipped
Chocolate Crumb Piecrust
Grated chocolate

Combine yolks, sugar, and salt in top of a double boiler. Gradually add milk, mixing well. Cook over boiling water, stirring constantly, until mixture coats a metal spoon. Soften gelatin in cold water; add to milk mixture, stirring well. Remove from heat and let cool. Stir in vanilla.

Beat egg whites (at room temperature) until stiff peaks form. Fold into gelatin mixture. Fold in whipped cream. Spoon filling into Chocolate Crumb Piecrust. Sprinkle with grated chocolate. Chill. Yield: one 10-inch pie.

Chocolate Crumb Piecrust:

2 cups chocolate wafer crumbs
½ cup butter or margarine, melted

Combine chocolate crumbs and butter, mixing well. Press firmly into bottom and sides of a greased 10-inch pieplate. Chill. Yield: one 10-inch piecrust.

VANILLA CHIFFON PIE

3 eggs, separated
½ cup sugar
¼ teaspoon salt
¼ teaspoon ground nutmeg
1½ cups milk, scalded
1 envelope unflavored gelatin
3 tablespoons cold water
½ teaspoon vanilla extract
1 baked (9-inch) pastry shell
1 cup whipping cream
2 tablespoons sugar
2 tablespoons grated chocolate

Combine egg yolks, ½ cup sugar, salt, and nutmeg in top of a double boiler, beating well. Gradually add milk, stirring constantly. Bring water in bottom of double boiler to a boil. Cook over boiling water, stirring constantly, until mixture is thickened. Soften gelatin in cold water; add to hot mixture, stirring well. Stir in vanilla. Set mixture aside to cool.

Beat egg whites (at room temperature) until stiff peaks form. Fold into cooled gelatin mixture. Pour filling into pastry shell. Chill until firm.

Beat whipping cream until foamy; gradually add 2 tablespoons sugar, beating until soft peaks form. Spread whipped cream over filling. Sprinkle with grated chocolate. Yield: one 9-inch pie.

CHOCOLATE RUM CREAM PIE

1¼ cups sugar, divided
1 package unflavored gelatin
Dash of salt
1 cup milk
2 eggs, separated
1 (6-ounce) package semisweet chocolate morsels
½ cup rum
1 teaspoon vanilla extract
1 baked (9-inch) pastry shell
½ cup whipping cream, whipped
Additional whipped cream (optional)

Combine 1 cup sugar, gelatin, and salt in a medium saucepan; add milk and egg yolks, stirring until well blended. Cook over medium heat, stirring constantly, 5 minutes or until slightly thickened. Remove from heat, and add chocolate morsels; stir until chocolate melts. Add rum and vanilla; chill until mixture is the consistency of unbeaten egg whites.

Beat egg whites (at room temperature) until foamy; gradually add remaining ¼ cup sugar, 1 tablespoon at a time, beating until stiff peaks form. Gently fold beaten egg whites into chilled chocolate mixture.

Spoon two-thirds of chocolate mixture into pastry shell; cover with ½ cup whipped cream. Dollop remaining chocolate mixture onto whipped cream; swirl chocolate and whipped cream together. Chill until set. Garnish with additional whipped cream, if desired. Yield: one 9-inch pie.

A 1920s ad for a reliable piecrust ingredient.

Delta Black Bottom Pie "bakes" perfectly in the refrigerator.

DELTA BLACK BOTTOM PIE

30 gingersnaps, crushed
½ cup butter or margarine,
  melted
¾ cup sugar
1 tablespoon plus ¾ teaspoon
  cornstarch
⅛ teaspoon salt
4 eggs, separated
2 cups milk, scalded
1½ (1-ounce) squares
  unsweetened chocolate
1 teaspoon vanilla extract
1 tablespoon unflavored
  gelatin
¼ cup cold water
2 tablespoons dark rum
¼ teaspoon cream of tartar
Grated chocolate (optional)
1 cup whipping cream,
  whipped

Combine cookie crumbs and butter, mixing well. Press firmly into bottom and sides of a lightly greased 10-inch pieplate. Bake at 300° for 10 minutes. Let cool completely.

Combine sugar, cornstarch, and salt in top of a double boiler. Beat egg yolks; add to sugar mixture, stirring well. Gradually add scalded milk. Bring water in bottom of double boiler to a boil. Reduce heat to low; cook, stirring constantly, until mixture is slightly thickened and coats a metal spoon. Remove from heat.

Remove 1¼ cups hot mixture; place in a small mixing bowl. Add chocolate squares; stir until chocolate melts. Cool slightly. Add vanilla; stir well. Pour filling into prepared piecrust. Chill until slightly set.

Dissolve gelatin in cold water; add to remaining hot mixture, stirring constantly. Let mixture cool. Stir in rum.

Beat egg whites (at room temperature) until foamy; add cream of tartar. Beat until stiff peaks form. Fold into cooled gelatin mixture. Spoon over chocolate mixture; chill until set. Sprinkle with grated chocolate, if desired. Pipe whipped cream around edge of pie with a pastry bag. Yield: one 10-inch pie.

General Electric's new round-topped refrigerator with a freezing compartment arrived in 1927 with recipes for several frozen desserts but no refrigerated gelatin-based pies. And since Mrs. S.R. Dull's up-to-date *Southern Cooking*, 1928, did not mention chiffon pies, we may assume that chiffon pies were a 1930s development. The 1942 *Good Housekeeping Cookbook* carried not only the lemon pie made with condensed milk, but also some fourteen genuine chiffon pies. (This is the book whose 1943 edition included the green-paged, waste-not "Wartime Supplement.") The busier the homemaker became, the more she relied on "bake" by refrigeration.

HIGH HAMPTON INN SUNNY SILVER PIE

4 eggs, separated
2 teaspoons grated lemon rind
3 tablespoons lemon juice
1 cup sugar, divided
1 envelope unflavored gelatin
⅓ cup cold water
Pinch of salt
1 baked (9-inch) pastry shell
1 cup whipping cream, whipped

Combine egg yolks, lemon rind and juice, and ½ cup sugar in top of a double boiler, mixing well. Bring water in bottom of double boiler to a boil. Cook, stirring constantly, until mixture thickens. Soften gelatin in cold water; add to lemon mixture, stirring well. Cool.

Beat egg whites (at room temperature) until foamy. Gradually add salt and remaining ½ cup sugar, 1 tablespoon at a time, beating until stiff peaks form. Fold egg whites into lemon mixture. Pour filling into pastry shell. Chill. Spread whipped cream over pie before serving. Yield: one 9-inch pie.

EGGNOG PIE

4 eggs, separated
1 cup sugar, divided
½ teaspoon salt
1 cup milk
1 envelope unflavored gelatin
¼ cup cold water
3 tablespoons bourbon or brandy
1 tablespoon rum
1 baked (9-inch) pastry shell
½ cup whipping cream
1 tablespoon rum

Combine egg yolks, ½ cup sugar, and salt in top of a double boiler; mix well. Gradually add milk, stirring constantly. Bring water in bottom of double boiler to a boil. Cook, stirring constantly, until mixture thickens. Soften gelatin in cold water; add to hot mixture, stirring well. Cool. Add bourbon and 1 tablespoon rum. Chill until mixture begins to thicken.

Beat egg whites (at room temperature) until foamy. Gradually add remaining ½ cup sugar, 1 tablespoon at a time, beating until stiff peaks form. Fold egg whites into cooled gelatin mixture. Pour filling into pastry shell. Chill.

Beat whipping cream until soft peaks form. Gradually add remaining 1 tablespoon rum, beating well. Serve pie with whipped cream. Yield: one 9-inch pie.

High Hampton Inn (inset), Cashiers, North Carolina. View from the porch is of the 8th green, an island surrounded by Hampton Lake.

By 1930 Graham crackers were a popular snack food.

LUSCIOUS LIME PIE

1½ envelopes unflavored
  gelatin
¾ cup sugar
¼ teaspoon salt
6 eggs, separated
¾ cup lime juice
¼ cup plus 2 tablespoons
  water
1½ teaspoons grated lime
  rind
4 to 5 drops green food
  coloring
¾ cup sugar
¾ cup whipping cream,
  whipped
2 baked (9-inch) coconut
  piecrusts
¾ cup whipping cream,
  whipped

Combine gelatin, ¾ cup sugar, and salt in a large saucepan. Beat egg yolks, lime juice, and water together; stir into gelatin mixture. Cook over low heat, stirring constantly, until mixture comes to a boil. Remove from heat; stir in lime rind and food coloring. Chill, stirring occasionally, until mixture begins to thicken.

Beat egg whites (at room temperature) until foamy. Gradually add ¾ cup sugar, 1 tablespoon at a time, beating until stiff peaks form. Fold into chilled gelatin mixture. Fold in ¾ cup whipped cream.

Pour mixture into piecrusts. Chill until firm. Garnish with ¾ cup whipped cream before serving. Yield: two 9-inch pies.

TART LEMON CHIFFON PIE

1 envelope unflavored gelatin
¼ cup cold water
4 eggs, separated
1¾ cups sugar, divided
1 tablespoon lemon rind
¾ cup fresh lemon juice
⅛ teaspoon salt
1 (9-inch) graham cracker
  piecrust
Whipped cream (optional)
Lemon slices (optional)

Soften gelatin in cold water; set aside.

Beat egg yolks until thick and lemon colored. Combine yolks, 1 cup sugar, lemon rind and juice, and salt in a saucepan; stir until smooth. Cook over medium heat, stirring constantly, 5 minutes or until thickened. Remove from heat; add gelatin. Stir well. Cool.

Beat egg whites (at room temperature) until foamy; gradually add remaining ¾ cup sugar, 1 tablespoon at a time, beating until soft peaks form.

Fold egg whites into lemon mixture; pour into piecrust. Chill. Garnish with whipped cream and lemon, if desired. Yield: one 9-inch pie.

NESSELRODE PIE

1 tablespoon unflavored
  gelatin
¼ cup cold water
2 eggs, separated
Pinch of salt
½ cup plus 2 tablespoons
  sugar, divided
2 cups half-and-half, scalded
1½ teaspoons rum extract
1 cup whipping cream,
  whipped
¼ cup chopped mixed candied
  fruit
¼ cup finely chopped pecans
1 baked (9-inch) pastry shell
½ cup whipping cream,
  whipped
Grated chocolate

Soften gelatin in cold water; set aside.

Combine egg yolks, salt, and ¼ cup sugar in top of a double boiler; beat well. Gradually add scalded half-and-half to yolk mixture, stirring constantly. Bring water in bottom of double boiler to a boil. Cook mixture over boiling water, stirring constantly, 5 minutes or until slightly thickened. Remove from heat; add softened gelatin. Stir until gelatin dissolves. Stir in rum extract. Chill until mixture reaches consistency of un- beaten egg whites.

Beat egg whites (at room tem- perature) until foamy. Gradually add remaining ¼ cup plus 2 ta- blespoons sugar, beating until stiff peaks form.

Fold egg whites, 1 cup whipped cream, candied fruit, and pecans into chilled gelatin mixture. Spoon filling into pastry shell. Chill 2 hours or until set.

Garnish with ½ cup whipped cream and grated chocolate. Yield: one 9-inch pie.

Savannah Christmas Rum Pie makes a celebration of any meal.

SAVANNAH CHRISTMAS RUM PIE

6 egg yolks
¾ cup sugar
¾ cup dark rum, divided
¼ cup water
1½ envelopes unflavored
  gelatin
3 cups whipping cream,
  whipped
2 (9-inch) graham cracker
  crumb piecrusts
Red and green candied
  cherries

Combine egg yolks and sugar; beat until thick and lemon col- ored. Set aside.

Combine ½ cup rum and water in a small saucepan; add gelatin, stirring to dissolve. Cook mixture over medium heat 5 minutes, stirring constantly. Remove from heat, and cool slightly.

Add cooled gelatin mixture to yolk mixture, stirring to blend well. Gradually fold into whipped cream. Fold in remain- ing ¼ cup rum. Spoon mixture evenly into piecrusts. Chill until set. Garnish with candied cher- ries. Yield: two 9-inch pies.

WEIDMANN'S SHERRY CHIFFON PIE

2 envelopes unflavored gelatin
⅓ cup cold water
4 eggs, separated
½ cup sugar
2 tablespoons sherry
½ teaspoon almond extract
1 cup sweetened condensed milk
1 (9-inch) graham cracker piecrust
Whipped cream
Toasted sliced almonds

Dissolve gelatin in cold water; set aside.

Beat egg yolks and sugar in a small mixing bowl until thick and lemon colored. Add dissolved gelatin, sherry, and almond extract; mix well.

Heat milk in a saucepan over medium heat until hot. Remove from heat; cool slightly. Add yolk mixture, stirring until well blended. Cool.

Beat egg whites (at room temperature) until stiff peaks form. Fold into cooled milk mixture, stirring until well blended. Pour filling into piecrust, and chill thoroughly. Garnish with whipped cream and toasted almonds. Yield: one 9-inch pie.

Trade card shows mother's helper rolling out the dough, a favored chore for children.

APRICOT CHIFFON PIE

2 envelopes unflavored gelatin
2 cups apricot nectar, divided
1¼ cups sugar, divided
1 tablespoon cornstarch
¼ teaspoon salt
1 (8-ounce) package cream cheese, softened
¼ teaspoon grated lemon rind
2 tablespoons lemon juice
1 cup whipping cream
2 (9-inch) graham cracker piecrusts

Soften gelatin in 1 cup apricot nectar; set aside.

Combine 1 cup sugar, cornstarch, salt, and remaining apricot nectar. Cook over medium heat, stirring constantly, until thickened. Remove from heat, and add gelatin mixture. Stir until gelatin dissolves; cool 30 minutes.

Beat cream cheese in a medium mixing bowl; gradually add cooled apricot mixture, lemon rind, and juice, beating until smooth. Chill mixture 30 minutes.

Beat whipping cream until foamy; gradually add remaining ¼ cup sugar, beating until stiff peaks form. Gently fold apricot mixture into whipped cream. Spoon filling evenly into piecrusts. Chill at least 3 hours. Yield: two 9-inch pies.

MEETING STREET FRESH FIG PIE

2 eggs, separated
¼ cup plus 2 tablespoons sugar, divided
⅛ teaspoon salt
¼ cup milk, scalded
3 envelopes unflavored gelatin
½ cup boiling water
1 tablespoon grated orange rind
2 tablespoons Triple Sec
½ cup whipping cream, whipped
2 cups ripe figs, peeled and diced
1 (9-inch) graham cracker piecrust

Combine egg yolks, ¼ cup sugar, and salt in a heavy saucepan; mix well. Gradually add scalded milk; cook over low heat 10 minutes or until thickened, stirring constantly. Soften gelatin in boiling water; add to custard mixture, stirring well. Stir in orange rind and Triple Sec. Set mixture aside to cool.

Beat egg whites (at room temperature) until foamy. Gradually add remaining sugar, 1 tablespoon at a time, beating until stiff peaks form. Fold egg whites, whipped cream, and figs into custard mixture. Pour filling into graham cracker piecrust. Chill 2 hours or until set. Yield: one 9-inch pie.

PUMPKIN CHIFFON PIE

¾ cup firmly packed brown sugar
1 envelope unflavored gelatin
½ teaspoon salt
1 teaspoon ground cinnamon
½ teaspoon ground nutmeg
¼ teaspoon ground ginger
3 eggs, separated
¾ cup milk
1¼ cups cooked, mashed pumpkin
⅓ cup sugar
1 baked (9-inch) pastry shell
Whipped cream
Chopped pecans

Combine brown sugar, gelatin, salt, cinnamon, nutmeg, and ginger in a heavy saucepan. Combine egg yolks and milk; beat well. Stir egg mixture into brown sugar mixture. Cook over medium heat, stirring constantly, until mixture comes to a boil. Remove from heat; stir in pumpkin. Chill until mixture begins to thicken.

Beat egg whites (at room temperature) until foamy. Gradually add ⅓ cup sugar, 1 tablespoon at a time, beating until stiff peaks form. Fold egg whites into chilled pumpkin mixture. Pour filling into pastry shell. Chill. Garnish with whipped cream and pecans before serving. Yield: one 9-inch pie.

A traveler in south central Mississippi said that he "ate sweet potatoes with wild turkeys and various other meats, had a potato pie for dessert and roasted potatoes offered to him as a side dish, drank sweet potato coffee and sweet potato home brew, had his horse fed on sweet potatoes and sweet potato vines, and when he retired he slept on a mattress stuffed with sweet potato vines and dreamed he was a sweet potato that someone was digging up."

From *Eating, Drinking, and Visiting in the South* by Joe Gray Taylor. 1982.

SWEET POTATO CHIFFON PIE

1 envelope unflavored gelatin
1¼ cups milk, divided
3 eggs, separated
⅔ cup sugar
¾ teaspoon ground cinnamon
1 cup cooked, mashed sweet potatoes
1 cup raisins
1 baked (9-inch) pastry shell
Whipped cream

Soften gelatin in ¼ cup milk; set aside.

Combine remaining 1 cup milk, egg yolks, sugar, cinnamon, sweet potatoes, and raisins in top of a double boiler, mixing well. Bring water in bottom of double boiler to a boil. Cook, stirring constantly, 10 minutes or until thickened. Remove from heat, and add gelatin mixture; stir well. Chill until slightly thickened.

Beat egg whites (at room temperature) until soft peaks form. Gently fold into sweet potato mixture. Spoon filling into pastry shell. Chill. Garnish with whipped cream before serving. Yield: one 9-inch pie.

Pixie power depicted in nineteenth-century advertising card.

ICEBOX PIES

CHOCOLATE ICEBOX PIE

⅔ cup sugar
¼ cup plus 1 tablespoon all-purpose flour
Dash of salt
2 (1-ounce) squares unsweetened chocolate, melted
1 (13-ounce) can evaporated milk
1 cup water
2 egg yolks, slightly beaten
2 cups miniature marshmallows
¼ cup butter or margarine
1 (9-inch) graham cracker piecrust
Whipped cream (optional)
1 tablespoon finely chopped pecans (optional)

Combine sugar, flour, and salt in a heavy saucepan. Mix well to remove lumps. Add chocolate; stir well. Gradually add milk, stirring constantly, to prevent lumps from forming. Add water and egg yolks; stir well.

Cook over low heat 15 minutes or until thickened, stirring frequently. Remove from heat, and stir in marshmallows and butter. Cool slightly. Pour filling into piecrust. Chill 4 hours or until firm. Garnish with whipped cream and pecans, if desired. Yield: one 9-inch pie.

In 1857, Gail Borden developed a process for canning milk, and soon he had patented and begun producing Eagle Brand Sweetened Condensed Milk. It played an important part in the development of formulas for infant feeding even before it was discovered that the acid in lemon or lime would cause it to solidify enough to be pie filling.

FRENCH SILK CHOCOLATE PIE

¾ cup butter or margarine, softened
1 cup sugar
3 (1-ounce) squares unsweetened chocolate, melted
1¼ teaspoons vanilla extract
3 eggs
1 baked (9-inch) pastry shell
Shaved chocolate (optional)
Chocolate leaves (optional)

Cream butter; gradually add sugar, beating with an electric mixer until light and fluffy. Add chocolate and vanilla; beat 5 minutes. Add eggs, one at a time, beating 5 minutes after each addition. Spoon filling into pastry shell. Chill at least 5 hours or until firm. Garnish with shaved chocolate and chocolate leaves, if desired. Yield: one 9-inch pie.

Waiting for the opening. Condensed milk trade card, late 1800s.

FLORIDA KEY LIME PIE

4 eggs, separated
1 (14-ounce) can sweetened condensed milk
½ cup Key lime juice
1 (9-inch) graham cracker piecrust
⅛ teaspoon cream of tartar
¼ cup plus 2 tablespoons sugar

Beat egg yolks in a medium mixing bowl until thick and lemon colored. Add milk and lime juice; blend well. Spoon filling into graham cracker piecrust.

Combine egg whites (at room temperature) and cream of tartar; beat until foamy. Gradually add sugar, 1 tablespoon at a time, beating until stiff peaks form. Spread meringue over filling, sealing to edge of piecrust. Bake at 350° for 10 minutes or until meringue is golden brown. Cool to room temperature. Chill. Yield: one 9-inch pie.

Collection of Business Americana

Old Southern Tea Room Lemon Icebox Pie with scalloped edges.

WEIDMANN'S BOURBON PIE

1 cup evaporated milk, scalded
21 large marshmallows
¼ cup bourbon
1 cup whipping cream, whipped
1 (9-inch) chocolate wafer piecrust
Additional whipped cream
Grated chocolate

Combine milk and marshmallows in a heavy saucepan. Cook over low heat, stirring constantly, until marshmallows melt. Do not let mixture boil. Stir in bourbon. Cool mixture completely.

Fold in 1 cup whipped cream. Pour mixture into piecrust. Chill at least 4 hours or overnight. Garnish with additional whipped cream and grated chocolate before serving. Yield: one 9-inch pie.

PEANUT BRITTLE PIE

18 large marshmallows
Pinch of salt
½ cup plus 2 tablespoons milk
1¼ cups finely crushed peanut brittle
1¼ cups whipping cream, whipped
1 (9-inch) graham cracker piecrust

Combine marshmallows, salt, and milk in top of a double boiler. Bring water in bottom of double boiler to a boil. Cook over boiling water, stirring frequently, until marshmallows melt and mixture is smooth. Cool 15 minutes. Add peanut brittle; stir well.

Carefully fold whipped cream into peanut brittle mixture; pour into graham cracker piecrust. Chill until firm. Yield: one 9-inch pie.

OLD SOUTHERN TEA ROOM LEMON ICEBOX PIE

1 cup vanilla wafer crumbs
2 tablespoons butter or margarine, melted
Vanilla wafers
1 (14-ounce) can sweetened condensed milk
4 eggs, separated
½ cup lemon juice
½ cup sugar

Combine vanilla wafer crumbs and butter; press into bottom of a lightly greased 9-inch pieplate. Line sides of pieplate with whole vanilla wafers; gently press into bottom layer.

Bake at 350° for 8 to 10 minutes. Cool.

Combine milk, egg yolks, and lemon juice; mix well. Pour into prepared pieplate.

Beat egg whites (at room temperature) until foamy. Gradually add sugar, 1 tablespoon at a time, beating until stiff peaks form. Spread meringue over filling, sealing to edge of piecrust. Bake at 350° for 10 minutes or until meringue is golden brown. Cool to room temperature. Chill. Yield: one 9-inch pie.

TEATIME TREATS

Tarts and Tartlets

T arts are individual-sized dessert servings, as differentiated from tartlets, which are those tiny pastries meant to be consumed in a couple of bites. The wee ones are traditionally the crown jewels of a party table. Tart tins about four inches wide are available in most department stores. Diminutive tartlet tins, made in France, can be purchased in cookware shops, but most Southern home cooks still use the miniature "gem" or muffin tins.

Our taste for such dainties as these goes back to the days of King Henry VIII, so one story goes, when Anne Boleyn baked some tarts for His Majesty while he was still married to Catherine of Aragon and Anne was her Maid of Honor. "Maids of Honor," a truly fine recipe, as usual, outlived its creator. Banbury Tarts are very old as well. They are so maddeningly delicious that they may well have been the tarts that made the Knave of Hearts into a petty criminal, although proof is difficult to come by. However, Banbury Tarts are technically turnovers; we have no record of their having been baked in open tart shells. Accordingly, our Banbury Tart recipe can be found with the turnovers on page 137.

For ease in handling, filled tart and tartlet tins are placed on cookie sheets to bake. Some cooks prefer, when baking empty shells, to place the pastry on the outside of the tins, trim the dough, and line them up on the sheets. Whether upside-down or right-side-up, tart shells must be pricked generously all over; lucky the cook who has an old-fashioned, sharp-tined "granny fork" for this purpose.

When crust and filling are to be baked together, as in chess tarts, the shells may be pricked and blind-baked, not browned, but enough to set the pastry. This precaution will prevent the filling from soaking into the crust.

One of the wonders of the world is the fact that it is possible to circumvent the above pastry-making operation by buying tart shells ready-made. They come in several sizes, available in specialty food sections. There are times in the lives of cooks when expediency has to take precedence over perfectionism.

With this chapter it is time to think smaller, smallest.

Original Overton family china sets a dessert table at Travellers' Rest, near Nashville. Chess Tarts, left (page 119), Peach Tartlets (page 122), and Petite Cherry Tarts (page 121) were as appropriate then as now.

APRICOT TARTS

¼ cup butter or margarine,
  softened
½ cup sugar, divided
2 teaspoons grated lemon
  rind
2 eggs, separated
1 (8¾-ounce) can apricot
  halves, undrained
⅓ cup all-purpose flour
¼ teaspoon baking powder
6 unbaked (4-inch) tart shells

Cream butter; gradually add ¼ cup sugar, beating until light and fluffy. Stir in lemon rind. Add egg yolks, one at a time, beating well after each addition.

Drain apricot halves, reserving 1 tablespoon syrup; set apricots aside. Add reserved apricot syrup to batter, stirring well.

Combine flour and baking powder; add to batter, beating well. Spoon filling into tart shells. Bake at 375° for 20 minutes or until lightly browned.

Place one apricot half on each tart. Beat egg whites (at room temperature) until foamy. Gradually add remaining sugar, 1 tablespoon at a time, beating until stiff peaks form and sugar dissolves. Spread meringue over apricots, sealing to edge of pastry. Bake at 350° for 8 minutes or until meringue is golden brown. Yield: 6 tarts.

Many varieties of berries may be used in making tarts.

Uncooked berries and fruits make beautiful open-faced tarts. Place a spoonful of filling in baked shells. (The filling for Sherry Tarts is good, substituting vanilla or a liqucur for sherry.) Arrange small berries on filling; slice bananas, kiwi, pineapple, and other large fruits. Glaze light colored fruits with melted apricot jam, strained; dark fruits with melted currant jelly.

BLUEBERRY TARTS

1 cup sugar
3 tablespoons cornstarch
2 tablespoons lemon juice
½ cup water
3 cups fresh blueberries or 1
  (16-ounce) package frozen
  blueberries, thawed and
  drained
6 baked (4-inch) tart shells
Whipped cream

Combine sugar, cornstarch, lemon juice, water, and blueberries in a heavy saucepan. Cook over low heat, stirring occasionally, 15 minutes or until thickened and bubbly. Cool.

Spoon mixture evenly into tart shells. Cool completely. Top with whipped cream before serving. Yield: 6 tarts.

GLAZED STRAWBERRY TARTS

1 cup sugar
3 tablespoons cornstarch
2 tablespoons water
¾ cup crushed fresh
  strawberries
1 teaspoon lemon juice
3 cups whole fresh
  strawberries
6 baked (2¾-inch) tart shells
Whipped cream

Combine sugar and cornstarch in a saucepan; stir in water. Add crushed strawberries and lemon juice; cook over low heat, stirring constantly, 10 minutes or until thickened and clear. Cool.

Place whole strawberries in tart shells. Pour glaze evenly over berries. Chill. Top with whipped cream before serving. Yield: 6 tarts.

LEMON MERINGUE TARTS

1 cup sugar
2 tablespoons cornstarch
3 eggs, separated
1 tablespoon butter or
  margarine, melted
Grated rind and juice of 1
  large lemon
Pinch of salt
1 cup water
6 baked (4-inch) tart shells
¼ cup plus 2 tablespoons
  sifted powdered sugar

Combine sugar and cornstarch in top of a double boiler, stirring well. Add egg yolks, butter, lemon rind and juice, salt, and water; beat with a wire whisk. Cook over boiling water until smooth and thickened, beating constantly with wire whisk. Remove from heat. Spoon mixture into tart shells.

Beat egg whites (at room temperature) until foamy. Gradually add powdered sugar, 1 tablespoon at a time, until stiff peaks form. Spread meringue over filling of each tart, sealing to edge of pastry. Bake at 350° for 6 minutes or until meringue is lightly browned. Cool before serving. Yield: 6 tarts.

Children pose with strawberries in a Louisiana fruit market.

LEMON TARTS

½ cup butter or margarine,
  softened
2 cups firmly packed brown
  sugar
12 egg yolks, slightly beaten
½ teaspoon lemon extract
8 unbaked (4-inch) tart shells

Combine butter, sugar, yolks, and lemon extract in a large mixing bowl; stir well.

Spoon mixture into tart shells. Bake at 350° for 25 minutes or until lightly browned. Yield: 8 tarts.

LIME CHIFFON TARTS

4 eggs, separated
1 cup sugar, divided
⅓ cup lime juice
½ teaspoon salt
1 envelope unflavored gelatin
¼ cup cold water
1 tablespoon grated lime rind
3 drops green food coloring
36 baked (2¾-inch) tart shells
Fresh mint sprigs (optional)

Beat egg yolks in top of a double boiler. Gradually add ½ cup sugar, lime juice, and salt, mixing well. Bring water to a boil. Reduce heat to medium; cook, stirring constantly, until thickened. Remove from heat.

Dissolve gelatin in cold water; add to yolk mixture, stirring until well blended. Stir in lime rind and food coloring. Cool.

Beat egg whites (at room temperature) until foamy. Add remaining ½ cup sugar, 1 tablespoon at a time, beating until stiff peaks form. Fold into lime mixture. Spoon 3 tablespoons filling into each tart shell. Chill. Garnish with fresh mint sprigs, if desired. Yield: 3 dozen tarts.

Lemon Variation:

Substitute ⅓ cup lemon juice and 1 tablespoon grated lemon rind for lime juice and rind. Substitute 1 to 2 drops yellow food coloring for green food coloring. Garnish with frosted grapes, if desired.

ORANGE-CHEESE TARTS

½ cup orange juice
1 package unflavored
  gelatin
½ cup milk
½ cup sugar
1 (8-ounce) package cream
  cheese, softened
2 cups fresh orange sections,
  seeded and well-drained
1 cup whipping cream
10 baked (4-inch) tart shells

Combine orange juice and gelatin in a small saucepan; stir well. Add milk and sugar, stirring well. Cook over low heat, stirring constantly with a wire whisk, 5 minutes or until sugar and gelatin dissolve. Cool slightly.

Beat cream cheese in a large mixing bowl until light and fluffy. Gradually add gelatin mixture, beating constantly. Fold in orange sections. Chill until mixture begins to thicken.

Beat whipping cream until soft peaks form. Fold into orange mixture. Spoon mixture evenly into tart shells. Chill until set. Yield: 10 tarts.

Note: Two (11-ounce) cans mandarin orange sections, well drained, may be substituted for fresh orange sections.

PUMPKIN CHIFFON TARTS

1 envelope unflavored gelatin
¼ cup boiling water
3 eggs, separated
1½ cups cooked, mashed
  pumpkin
1 cup firmly packed brown
  sugar
1 teaspoon ground
  cinnamon
½ teaspoon ground allspice
½ teaspoon ground ginger
½ teaspoon salt
2 tablespoons sugar
10 baked (4-inch) tart shells
Whipped cream (optional)

Soften gelatin in boiling water; set aside.

Beat egg yolks in top of a double boiler. Add pumpkin, brown sugar, spices, and salt, mixing well. Cook over boiling water, stirring occasionally, until thoroughly heated. Add gelatin mixture, mixing well. Chill until mixture mounds when dropped from a spoon.

Beat egg whites (at room temperature) until foamy. Gradually add sugar, beating until stiff peaks form. Fold into pumpkin mixture. Spoon mixture evenly into tart shells. Chill until firm. Garnish with whipped cream, if desired. Yield: 10 tarts.

Label of a Louisiana orange grower.

Boiling down sugarcane is a social activity for families and neighbors.

BROWN SUGAR TARTS

½ cup butter or margarine, softened
1 cup firmly packed brown sugar
2 eggs
1 cup raisins
1 cup chopped pecans
1 teaspoon ground cinnamon
1 teaspoon vanilla extract
10 unbaked (2¾-inch) tart shells
Whipped cream (optional)

Cream butter; gradually add sugar, beating well. Add eggs, one at a time, beating well after each addition. Stir in raisins, pecans, cinnamon, and vanilla.

Spoon 2 tablespoons filling into each tart shell. Bake at 350° for 20 minutes. Cool. Garnish with whipped cream, if desired. Yield: 10 tarts.

CARAMEL CREAM TARTS

4 egg yolks, slightly beaten
2 cups firmly packed brown sugar
¼ cup plus 2 tablespoons all-purpose flour
2 cups water
1 tablespoon plus 1 teaspoon butter or margarine
1½ teaspoons vanilla extract
6 baked (4-inch) tart shells
Whipped cream

Combine yolks, sugar, flour, and water in top of a double boiler; stir until smooth. Place over boiling water; reduce heat to low, and cook until thickened, stirring frequently. Remove from heat; stir in butter and vanilla.

Spoon ½ cup filling into each tart shell. Chill. Garnish with whipped cream. Yield: 6 tarts.

CHESS TARTS

½ cup butter or margarine, softened
2 cups sugar
4 eggs
2 tablespoons plus 1½ teaspoons all-purpose flour
⅔ cup buttermilk
1 teaspoon vanilla extract
Pinch of salt
20 unbaked (2¾-inch) tart shells

Cream butter in a large mixing bowl; gradually add sugar, beating well. Add eggs, one at a time, beating well after each addition. Add flour, buttermilk, vanilla, and salt, mixing well.

Spoon ¼ cup filling into each tart shell. Bake at 350° for 30 minutes. Yield: 20 tarts.

SHERRY TARTS

⅓ cup sugar
⅓ cup all-purpose flour
⅛ teaspoon salt
2 eggs, beaten
2 cups whipping cream, divided
½ cup milk
3 tablespoons sherry
6 baked (4-inch) tart shells
1 teaspoon sugar
Ground nutmeg (optional)

Combine ⅓ cup sugar, flour, and salt in top of a double boiler; stir to remove lumps. Add eggs, stirring well.

Scald 1½ cups whipping cream and milk; refrigerate remaining whipping cream. Gradually add hot cream mixture to egg mixture, stirring constantly. Cook over boiling water, stirring constantly, 10 minutes or until thickened. Cool. Stir in sherry. Spoon mixture into tart shells. Chill.

Beat reserved whipping cream until foamy. Add sugar; beat until stiff peaks form. Top each tart with whipped cream; sprinkle with nutmeg, if desired. Yield: 6 tarts.

To fill such a large pie will take a lot of Atmore's Mince Meat. Trade card.

MAIDS OF HONOR

2 eggs
½ cup sugar
2 tablespoons all-purpose flour
½ cup almond paste
2 tablespoons butter or margarine, melted
1 tablespoon lemon juice
1 tablespoon sherry
Strawberry or raspberry jam
8 unbaked (2¾-inch) tart shells

Beat eggs until thick and lemon colored; add sugar and flour, beating until smooth. Crumble almond paste into very small pieces; add to egg mixture. Stir in butter, lemon juice, and sherry, mixing well.

Place 1 teaspoon jam in each tart shell; spoon batter over jam in tart shells. Bake at 350° for 35 minutes or until lightly browned. Yield: 8 tarts.

MINCEMEAT TARTS FLAMBE

1 cup sugar
1 cup peeled, finely chopped apples
1 cup cooked, drained, and crumbled ground chuck
½ cup chopped raisins
¼ cup butter or margarine
1 tablespoon molasses
½ teaspoon salt
1 teaspoon ground cinnamon
Pinch of ground nutmeg
Pinch of ground mace
Pinch of ground cloves
¼ cup brandy
6 baked (2¾-inch) tart shells
Whipped cream

Combine sugar, apples, ground chuck, raisins, butter, molasses, salt, and spices in a small Dutch oven. Cook over low heat, stirring frequently, until butter melts. Simmer an additional 30 minutes, stirring frequently. Spoon mixture into a chafing dish.

Place brandy in a small, long-handled pan; heat just until warm. Pour brandy over mincemeat, and ignite with a long match. Stir mixture gently until flames die down.

Spoon warm mincemeat mixture into tart shells; serve with whipped cream. Yield: 6 tarts.

Sherry Tarts with just a hint of wine to perk up the taste.

TARTLETS

PETITE CHERRY TARTS

4 cups fresh cherries, pitted
1½ cups sugar
¼ cup cornstarch
1 tablespoon water
¼ cup butter or margarine, softened
1 teaspoon almond extract
48 baked (1¾-inch) tart shells

Combine cherries and sugar in a large saucepan; cook over medium heat, stirring constantly, 15 minutes or until cherries are soft.

Dissolve cornstarch in water; blend well. Add to cherry mixture; bring to a boil. Reduce heat; cook, stirring constantly, until mixture is thickened and bubbly. Remove from heat, and stir in butter and almond extract. Cool. Spoon 2 teaspoons cherry filling into each tart shell. Yield: 4 dozen tarts.

The highlight of the Southern party table: melt-in-the-mouth sweet tartlets! We do have a couple of tiny tarts we call tassies, but a rose is a rose; Pecan Tassies and Martha White's Teatime Tassies are among the jewels we serve at almost any occasion.

Basket of Cherries, *by Atlanta, Georgia, seamstress Willie M. Chambers.*

Springtime in Georgia *by folk artist Mattie Lou O'Kelly.*

PEACH TARTLETS

1 cup peeled fresh peaches,
 diced
¼ cup plus 3 tablespoons
 sugar
1 tablespoon cornstarch
1½ teaspoons butter or
 margarine, softened
⅛ teaspoon almond extract
24 baked (1¾-inch) tart
 shells

Combine peaches and sugar in a saucepan; let stand 30 minutes or until mixture becomes syrupy. Cook over medium-low heat for 30 minutes.

Combine cornstarch and a small amount of water to form a smooth paste. Stir cornstarch mixture into peaches; bring to a boil. Reduce heat; cook, stirring constantly, until mixture becomes thickened and bubbly.

Remove from heat, and stir in butter and almond extract. Cool slightly. Spoon 2 teaspoons peach mixture into each tart shell. Yield: 2 dozen tarts.

CHEESE TARTLETS

2 cups graham cracker
 crumbs
½ cup butter or margarine,
 melted
2 tablespoons sugar
2 (3-ounce) packages cream
 cheese, softened
¼ cup sugar
1 egg, separated
¼ teaspoon vanilla extract
¼ cup commercial sour
 cream
1 tablespoon sugar
¼ teaspoon vanilla
 extract

Combine cracker crumbs, butter, and 2 tablespoons sugar; mix well. Fill each of 48 miniature 1¾-inch muffin tins with 1½ teaspoons crumb mixture. Press mixture firmly into bottom and sides of muffin tins.

Combine cream cheese and ¼ cup sugar in a medium mixing bowl; beat well. Add egg yolk and ¼ teaspoon vanilla, beating until well blended. Beat egg white (at room temperature) until stiff peaks form. Fold into cheese mixture. Spoon 1 teaspoon cheese mixture into each shell. Bake at 350° for 15 minutes. Remove from oven.

Combine sour cream, 1 tablespoon sugar, and ¼ teaspoon vanilla; mix well. Spoon ½ teaspoon topping on each tart. Bake at 350° for 5 minutes. Remove from tins; cool on wire racks. Yield: 4 dozen tarts.

One of the Southeast's oldest producers of cornmeal, flour, and convenience mix products is Martha White Foods, Inc. The story began in 1899, when the owner of Nashville's Royal Flour Mill named his leading flour for his three-year-old daughter, Martha White Lindsey. The child's picture still appears as a familiar trademark on every package the company sells. Martha White Foods, Inc., pioneered development of self-rising flour and cornmeal. They also were responsible for repackaging flour, originally available only by the barrel, in nickel and dime quantities; this less expensive, more convenient packaging was to set the standards for the entire industry.

MARTHA WHITE'S TEATIME TASSIES

Cream Cheese Pastry
1 tablespoon butter or margarine, softened
¾ cup firmly packed brown sugar
1 egg
1 teaspoon vanilla extract
⅛ teaspoon salt
½ cup coarsely chopped pecans

Divide pastry into 24 balls. Place each ball in an ungreased 1¾-inch muffin tin; press into tins to form shells. Set aside.

Cream butter; gradually add sugar, beating well. Add egg, vanilla, and salt; beat well. Stir in pecans. Spoon 1½ teaspoons filling into each tart shell. Bake at 350° for 25 minutes. Cool completely in pans. Yield: 2 dozen tarts.

Cream Cheese Pastry:

1 (3-ounce) package cream cheese, softened
½ cup butter or margarine, softened
1 cup all-purpose flour

Combine cream cheese and butter; cream until smooth. Add flour, mixing well. Chill dough at least 2 hours. Yield: pastry for 2 dozen 1¾-inch tarts.

Martha White's Teatime Tassies for an afternoon pick-me-up.

Dates pictured in a print from The Grocer's Encyclopedia by Artemis Ward.

MINIATURE DATE-PECAN TARTS

1 (3-ounce) package cream
  cheese, softened
½ cup butter or margarine,
  softened
1 cup all-purpose flour
½ cup butter or margarine,
  softened
1 cup sugar
2 eggs, separated
1 cup finely chopped dates
1 cup chopped pecans
1 teaspoon vanilla extract

Combine cream cheese, butter, and flour; mix well. Shape dough into 1-inch balls; press into 48 miniature 1¾-inch muffin tins to form shells.

Cream butter and sugar in a medium mixing bowl; add egg yolks, beating well. Stir in dates, pecans, and vanilla.

Beat egg whites (at room temperature) until stiff peaks form. Gently fold egg whites into batter. Spoon 1½ teaspoons batter into each prepared shell.

Bake at 325° for 25 minutes. Remove from pans while warm. Cool on wire racks. Yield: 4 dozen tarts.

PECAN TASSIES

½ cup butter or margarine,
  softened
1 cup firmly packed brown
  sugar
1 egg
¼ teaspoon salt
½ cup coarsely chopped
  pecans
36 unbaked (1¾-inch) tart
  shells

Cream butter; gradually add sugar, beating well. Add egg and salt, beating well. Stir in pecans. Spoon 1½ teaspoons filling into each tart shell. Bake at 350° for 30 minutes. Remove from pans while warm; cool on wire racks. Yield: 3 dozen tarts.

L ining standard-sized tart tins is no problem; any good flaky pastry will work. But lining the little gem pans necessary for making bite-size tarts, is a bit trickier. Pâte Brisée Sucrée (sweet paste) is ideal for the purpose, as it does not shrink in baking and, since it is crisp (not necessarily flaky), it can be handled without damage. Pastries containing egg or cream cheese can also take more handling than flaky ones. Once the pastry is mixed, individual lumps of dough may be pinched off, rolled into balls, and pressed into the small tins to form shells. The method for this kind of pastry shell will be found with Martha White's Teatime Tassies or with Miniature Date-Pecan Tarts; however, it is suitable to use with any of the recipes in this section.

DAINTY LEMON TARTS

2 cups sugar
1½ teaspoons grated
   lemon rind
½ cup lemon juice
1 cup butter or
   margarine
4 eggs, beaten
Tart shells (recipe follows)
Whipped cream (optional)
Blueberries (optional)

Combine first 4 ingredients in top of a double boiler; bring water to a boil. Reduce heat to low and cook, stirring constantly, until butter melts.

Gradually stir about one-fourth of hot mixture into eggs; add to remaining hot mixture, stirring constantly. Cook in top of double boiler, stirring constantly, 20 minutes or until thickened. Chill 2 hours. Spoon 1 teaspoon filling into each tart shell. Garnish each tart with whipped cream and blueberries, if desired. Yield: about 8 dozen.

Tart Shells:

3 cups all-purpose
   flour
1½ teaspoons salt
1 cup shortening
5 to 6 tablespoons
   ice water

Combine flour and salt in a large mixing bowl; cut in shortening with a pastry blender until mixture resembles coarse meal. Sprinkle water evenly over surface of flour mixture; stir with a fork until dry ingredients are moistened. Shape dough into a ball; chill.

Roll dough to ⅛-inch thickness on a lightly floured surface; cut into rounds with a 2-inch scalloped cutter. Fit each pastry into a 1¾-inch muffin pan; prick each with a fork. Bake at 400° for 10 to 12 minutes. Yield: about 8 dozen tarts.

Virginia Dare brand flavor extracts used a happy child to carry advertising message. We still use miniature gem pans just like the one pictured.

M arion Flexner, author of *Out of Kentucky Kitchens*, 1949, began cooking at age three; at least that is what her family remembered. The family cook would put a crisp white apron over her head and allow her to "cook"; that is how she learned the feel of doughs and the "cook-taste method."

Mother always uses VIRGINIA DARE *Double Strength* Extracts... It requires only half the quantity

LITTLE PASTRIES

Dumplings, Fried Pies, and Turnovers

J ust about every cuisine has its dumplings, some savory, some sweet: Russian vareniki, Polish piroshki, Chinese won ton, South American empanadas — the latter when filled with a sweet is empanada dulce, and there is a recipe for it in this chapter. Large English puddings were wrapped in cloth which had been dampened and heavily floured to keep the pudding from absorbing water. The tradition crossed the ocean with the settlers. A boiled dumpling is, after all, but a small version of our ancient boiled pudding heritage. Dumplings may be baked, of course, and sometimes the cook will pour water or syrup around them in the pan.

Depending upon which area he comes from, a Southerner will call a fried pie a half moon, a mule ear, or even a crab lantern. Usually filled with dried fruit, fried pies were a sweet reward for all the hard work that took place when the fruit was harvested in the fall. In those old days, women got together for apple bees or peach bees, peeling and slicing for hours. Then followed the tedious task of guarding the drying fruit from rain and insects. Dried fruit was precious in winter, fried pies the ultimate use for it.

Some cooks will encase the filling in plain pastry, while others use their regular biscuit dough on the principle that the pie will absorb fat in the frying. But there is a recipe for an evaporated milk pastry in this chapter that comes from Texas via Arkansas that seems to strike just the right note for pies to be fried.

Turnovers, to round out our small pastries, are tasty little morsels, variously filled, folded, and baked. They're nice for teatime, and we cut the pastry smaller for party food than for dessert servings. Cream cheese in the pastry results in a tender, rich wrap for marmalade or jam for the tea tray. Banbury turnovers are usually called tarts, but, since they are enclosed in a triangle of dough and baked, they belong in the company of other turnovers; ground-up raisins and lemons give them a flavor like no other. Turnovers, as you will see, may be shaped into half-circles, triangles, or rectangles — cook's option!

Mother's Peach Dumplings (page 130) are in soup bowl with syrup. Platter holds Cream Cheese Pastries (page 135) and Fried Apple Pies (page 132). A few examples of good things in small packages.

DUMPLINGS

Baked Apple Dumplings with sweet syrup underneath.

BAKED APPLE DUMPLINGS

Pastry for 1 double-crust
  (9-inch) pie
6 medium-size cooking
  apples, peeled and cored
½ cup sugar
1½ teaspoons ground
  cinnamon
Butter or margarine
2 cups water
1 cup sugar
3 tablespoons butter or
  margarine
¼ teaspoon ground cinnamon

Roll dough to ¼-inch thickness on a lightly floured surface; shape into a 24- x 16-inch rectangle. Cut into six 8-inch squares. Reserve excess pastry.

Place an apple in center of each pastry square. Combine ½ cup sugar and 1½ teaspoons cinnamon, mixing well. Fill core of each apple with sugar mixture; dot with butter. Moisten edges of each pastry square with water; bring corners to center, pinching edges to seal. Place dumplings in a 13- x 9- x 2-inch baking dish. Roll out reserved pastry; cut into decorative shapes, and arrange on top of dumplings, if desired.

Combine water, 1 cup sugar, 3 tablespoons butter, and ¼ teaspoon cinnamon in a heavy saucepan; bring to a boil. Continue to boil 3 minutes, stirring frequently. Pour syrup around dumplings.

Bake at 425° for 40 minutes or until crust is browned and apples are soft. Serve warm. Yield: 6 dumplings.

B oiled dumplings were preferred by many; an Ozark Mountain woman remembered: "We children called them 'Good ole Dishrag' because they were wrapped in squares of muslin." They were always served with a thin milk mixture called "dip," an all-purpose dessert sauce widely known and used throughout the South. When serving dumplings, either baked or boiled, with sauce or "dip," put them into soup plates to contain all the sweet juices.

BOILED APPLE DUMPLINGS

4 cups all-purpose flour
2 tablespoons sugar
1 teaspoon salt
1 teaspoon baking soda
½ cup butter or margarine
2 cups buttermilk
8 medium-size cooking
  apples, peeled and cored
5 tablespoons plus 1
  teaspoon sugar, divided
2 tablespoons plus 2
  teaspoons butter or
  margarine, divided
1 teaspoon ground
  cinnamon, divided
Cheesecloth
½ cup butter or margarine,
  divided
Dip (recipe follows)

Combine flour, 2 tablespoons sugar, salt, and baking soda in a large mixing bowl. Cut in ½ cup butter with a pastry blender until mixture resembles coarse meal. Add 2 cups buttermilk, stirring until dry ingredients are moistened.

Divide dough into 8 equal portions. Roll each portion into a 6-inch circle on a lightly floured surface. Place an apple on each circle. Fill each apple center with 2 teaspoons sugar, 1 teaspoon butter, and ⅛ teaspoon cinnamon. Moisten edges of dough with water. Fold dough over apple; pinch edges together to seal. Wrap each dumpling in a 12-inch square of cheesecloth; tie securely.

Place dumplings in a large Dutch oven with boiling salted water to cover. Simmer 35 to 40 minutes. Remove dumplings; discard cheesecloth. Place each dumpling in an individual serving bowl; top each with 1 tablespoon butter. Serve dumplings hot with dip. Yield: 8 servings.

Dip:

2 cups milk
1 tablespoon whipping cream
¼ cup sugar
½ teaspoon ground cinnamon
¼ teaspoon ground nutmeg

Combine all ingredients; stir well. Chill. Stir vigorously before serving. Yield: about 2 cups.

Apple harvesting was a community event. West Virginia, 1910.

BLACKBERRY DUMPLINGS

5 cups fresh blackberries
4 cups water
2½ cups sugar
1 cup milk
1 cup sugar
¼ cup butter or margarine,
   melted and cooled
2 eggs, beaten
2 teaspoons vanilla extract
3½ cups all-purpose flour
1 tablespoon baking
   powder
Vanilla ice cream

Combine blackberries, water, and 2½ cups sugar in a large Dutch oven; stir well. Cook over medium heat until mixture comes to a boil.

Combine milk, 1 cup sugar, butter, eggs, and vanilla in a large mixing bowl; mix well. Combine flour and baking powder, stirring well. Gradually add flour mixture to milk mixture, stirring lightly until dry ingredients are moistened and a soft dough forms.

Drop dough by teaspoonfuls into boiling blackberry mixture. Cook 2 to 3 minutes or until dumplings rise to surface and center of dumplings test done when pierced with a wooden pick. Transfer dumplings to individual serving bowls, using a slotted spoon. Spoon blackberry mixture over dumplings, and serve warm with vanilla ice cream. Yield: 12 to 15 servings.

MOTHER'S PEACH DUMPLINGS

Pastry (recipe follows)
8 fresh peaches, peeled,
   pitted, and cut in half
½ cup sugar
2 teaspoons ground
   cinnamon
Butter or margarine
Syrup (recipe follows)
½ teaspoon vanilla extract

Divide pastry into 8 equal portions; roll each to ¼-inch thickness on a lightly floured surface. Trim edges to form a square.

Place 1 peach half, cut side up, in center of each pastry square. Combine sugar and cinnamon; spoon 1 tablespoon of sugar mixture into center of each peach half. Dot with butter. Place remaining peach halves, cut side down, over sugar mixture. Moisten edges of each dumpling with water; bring corners to center, pinching edges to seal. Place dumplings, seam side down, in a lightly greased 13- x 9- x 2-inch baking dish.

Bake at 450° for 15 minutes or until lightly browned. Reduce heat to 300°; pour half of syrup over dumplings. Stir vanilla into remaining syrup. Bake an additional 30 minutes, gradually adding additional syrup so dumplings will not bake dry. Yield: 8 servings.

Pastry:

3 cups all-purpose flour
1 tablespoon baking powder
1½ teaspoons salt
1 cup plus 2 tablespoons
   shortening
¾ cup milk

Combine flour, baking powder, and salt in a medium mixing bowl. Cut in shortening with a pastry blender until mixture resembles coarse meal. Gradually add milk, stirring to make a soft dough. Yield: pastry for 8 dumplings.

Syrup:

1½ cups sugar
¾ cup hot water
¼ cup light corn syrup
1 tablespoon butter or
   margarine
Pinch of salt

Combine sugar, water, syrup, butter, and salt in a small saucepan; cook, stirring constantly, until mixture comes to a boil. Yield: 2½ cups.

In the 1920s and 1930s, wild blackberries grew in profusion in the rural South, and pails filled rapidly.

North Carolina Collection, University of North Carolina Library, Chapel Hill

THE TWO PEACHES.

See the Two Peaches on the Tree.

They are Discussing their future.

One is a Green Peach who doesn't know much, and he says he would like to be Plucked and Skinned by a Millionaire.

But the other Peach, who is not so Green and who has a Blooming Cheek, says he would like to be sweet and good and get into a Cottolene Dumpling.

Thus we see, "Cottolene Is The Best Policy."

FRIED PIES

FRIED APPLE PIES

2 (6-ounce) packages dried
  apple slices
1 cup sugar
1 teaspoon ground
  cinnamon
Pastry (recipe follows)
Vegetable oil

Place dried apple slices with water to cover in a medium saucepan. Bring to a boil; reduce heat, and simmer 30 minutes. Add sugar, and simmer an additional 30 minutes. Drain apples well, and mash. Stir cinnamon into mixture.

Roll dough to ¼-inch thickness on a lightly floured surface. Cut into 4-inch circles or squares.

Place 1 tablespoon apple mixture in center of each pastry circle. Moisten edges of pastry; fold in half, making sure edges are even. Press pastry edges firmly together using a fork dipped in flour.

Heat 1 inch of oil to 375° in a large skillet. Cook pies until golden brown on both sides, turning once. Drain well on paper towels. Yield: 2 dozen.

Pastry:

1 (13-ounce) can evaporated
  milk
1 egg, beaten
5 cups all-purpose
  flour
1 tablespoon salt
1 tablespoon sugar
1 cup shortening

Combine milk and egg; stir well. Set aside.

Combine flour, salt, and sugar in a large mixing bowl; cut in shortening with a pastry blender until mixture resembles coarse meal. Sprinkle milk mixture over flour mixture; stir with a fork until dry ingredients are moistened. Shape dough into a ball, and wrap in waxed paper. Chill at least 1 hour or until ready to use. Yield: pastry for 2 dozen 4-inch pies.

FRIED APRICOT PIES

2 (6-ounce) packages dried
  apricots
½ cup sugar
1 tablespoon lemon juice
½ teaspoon ground
  cinnamon
½ teaspoon ground
  nutmeg
Pastry (recipe follows)
Vegetable oil
Sifted powdered sugar
  (optional)

Place apricots with water to cover in a medium saucepan. Bring to a boil; reduce heat, and simmer 30 minutes. Drain well, and mash. Stir in sugar, lemon juice, cinnamon, and nutmeg; set aside.

Roll dough to ¼-inch thickness on a lightly floured surface. Cut into 4-inch circles.

Place 1 tablespoon apricot mixture in center of each pastry circle. Moisten edges of pastry; fold in half, making sure edges are even. Press pastry edges firmly together using a fork dipped in flour.

Heat 1 inch of oil to 375° in a large skillet. Cook pies until golden brown on both sides, turning once. Drain well on paper towels. Sprinkle with powdered sugar, if desired. Yield: 2 dozen.

Pastry:

3 cups all-purpose
  flour
1 teaspoon salt
¾ cup shortening
1 egg, beaten
¼ cup water
1 teaspoon vinegar

Combine flour and salt in a large mixing bowl; cut in shortening with a pastry blender until mixture resembles coarse meal. Combine egg and water; sprinkle over flour mixture. Add vinegar, and lightly stir with a fork until mixture forms a ball.

Wrap pastry in waxed paper; chill at least 1 hour or until ready to use. Yield: pastry for 2 dozen 4-inch pies.

Fried Apricot Pies: Dried fruit is best for the purpose.

Apricots, *from turn-of-the-century* Encyclopedia of Food.

Rolling out the dough. Trade card, 1800s.

Staples & Charles

FRIED PEACH PIES

1 (8-ounce) package dried
  peaches
⅓ cup sugar
1 tablespoon lemon juice
¼ teaspoon ground cinnamon
⅛ teaspoon ground nutmeg
Pastry (recipe follows)
Vegetable oil

Place peaches with water to cover in a large saucepan. Bring to a boil; reduce heat and simmer 1 hour. Drain peaches; reserve ¼ cup liquid. Mash peaches.

Combine peaches, reserved liquid, sugar, lemon juice, cinnamon, and nutmeg; stir well, and set aside.

Divide pastry into 24 portions. Roll each portion into a 3-inch circle on a lightly floured surface.

Place 1 tablespoon peach mixture in center of each pastry circle. Moisten edges of circles; fold pastry in half, making sure edges are even. Using a fork dipped in flour, press edges of pastry together to seal. Prick pastry 2 to 3 times.

Heat 1 inch of oil to 375°. Cook pies until golden brown, turning once. Drain well. Yield: 2 dozen.

Pastry:

2½ cups all-purpose flour
1 tablespoon sugar
1 tablespoon baking powder
1 teaspoon salt
⅓ cup shortening
1 egg, beaten
¾ cup plus 1 tablespoon
  evaporated milk

Combine dry ingredients; cut in shortening with a pastry blender until mixture resembles coarse meal. Combine egg and milk; stir into flour mixture with a fork until all ingredients are moistened. Cover, and chill 24 hours. Yield: pastry for 2 dozen 3-inch pies.

SOUTHERN FRIED CRANBERRY PIES

1½ cups fresh cranberries
¾ cup sugar
¼ cup water
1 tablespoon quick-cooking
  tapioca
1 tablespoon butter or
  margarine, softened
Pastry (recipe follows)
Vegetable oil
Sifted powdered sugar

Combine cranberries, sugar, water, and tapioca in a medium saucepan; let stand 5 minutes. Bring to a boil; reduce heat. Cook mixture over medium heat, stirring constantly, until thickened. Stir in butter. Set aside to cool.

Divide pastry into thirds; roll each portion to ⅛-inch thickness on waxed paper. Cut into 3½-inch circles.

Place 1 teaspoon cranberry mixture in center of each pastry circle. Moisten edges of pastry; fold in half, making sure edges are even. Press pastry edges firmly together using a fork dipped in flour.

Heat 2 to 3 inches of oil to 375° in a large skillet. Cook pies 4 to 5 at a time until golden brown on both sides, turning once. Drain well on paper towels. Sprinkle with powdered sugar. Yield: 2 dozen.

Pastry:

3 cups all-purpose
  flour
2 teaspoons baking
  powder
1 teaspoon salt
⅔ cup shortening
½ cup cold water

Combine flour, baking powder, and salt in a large mixing bowl; cut in shortening with a pastry blender until mixture resembles coarse meal. Sprinkle water over flour mixture; stir with a fork until dry ingredients are moistened. Shape dough into a ball, and wrap in waxed paper. Chill dough at least 1 hour or until ready to use. Yield: pastry for 2 dozen 3½-inch pies.

TURNOVERS

SUGAR PIES

Leftover pastry
2 tablespoons butter or
  margarine, melted
2 tablespoons sugar
¼ teaspoon ground cinnamon

Roll pastry into a 12- x 8-inch rectangle on a lightly floured surface.

Combine butter, sugar, and cinnamon; mix well. Brush over surface of pastry, leaving a ½-inch margin on all edges. Moisten edges with water; fold dough in half lengthwise. Press pastry edges together using a fork dipped in flour.

Transfer to a lightly greased baking sheet. Bake at 450° for 8 minutes or until golden brown. Cool slightly, and cut into ½-inch slices. Yield: 2 dozen.

APPLESAUCE TURNOVERS

2 cups all-purpose flour
1 teaspoon salt
1 teaspoon baking powder
1 teaspoon sugar
2 tablespoons butter or
  margarine
½ cup milk
½ cup applesauce
¼ cup sugar
½ teaspoon ground cinnamon

Combine first 4 ingredients in a medium mixing bowl. Cut in butter with a pastry blender. Gradually add milk, stirring until dry ingredients are moistened. Roll pastry to ⅛-inch thickness on a lightly floured surface. Cut into 4-inch squares or circles.

Combine applesauce, ¼ cup sugar, and cinnamon in a small mixing bowl. Place a heaping teaspoon of applesauce mixture in center of each pastry. Moisten edges with water; fold pastry in half. Press pastry edges firmly together with a fork dipped in flour.

Place on greased baking sheets. Bake at 425° for 10 minutes or until lightly browned. Yield: 30 turnovers.

CREAM CHEESE PASTRIES

1 cup butter or margarine,
  softened
2 (3-ounce) packages cream
  cheese, softened
2 cups all-purpose flour
¼ cup whipping cream
About 1¼ cups strawberry
  jam
1 egg, beaten
Sifted powdered sugar

Combine butter and cream cheese in a small mixing bowl; beat until smooth. Add flour, mixing well. Stir in whipping cream. Shape dough into a ball; chill 1 hour.

Roll pastry to ⅛-inch thickness on a lightly floured surface. Cut pastry into 48 (2¾-inch) rounds. Place 1 teaspoon strawberry jam in center of 24 pastry rounds. Top jam-filled pastries with remaining rounds. Moisten edges of pastry; fold in half, making sure edges are even. Press pastry edges firmly together using a fork dipped in flour. Prick tops with fork; brush with egg white, and sprinkle with powdered sugar.

Bake pastries on greased baking sheets at 425° for 15 minutes or until lightly browned. Yield: 2 dozen pastries.

Early stereo photo shows final preparation of sugar for market, the filling and sewing up of sugar bags.

TEA TURNOVERS

½ cup butter or margarine,
  softened
1 (3-ounce) package
  cream cheese,
  softened
1 cup all-purpose flour
¼ cup fruit preserves

Combine butter and cream
cheese in a small mixing bowl;
mix well. Stir in flour just until
blended. Shape dough into a
ball; cover and chill.

Roll pastry to ¼-inch thickness on a lightly floured surface.
Cut dough with a 3-inch biscuit
cutter. Place 1 teaspoon preserves in center of each pastry
circle. Moisten edges of pastry;
fold in half, making sure edges
are even. Press pastry edges
firmly together using a fork
dipped in flour.

Bake at 350° for 15 minutes
or until lightly browned. Place
on wire racks to cool. Yield: 1
dozen turnovers.

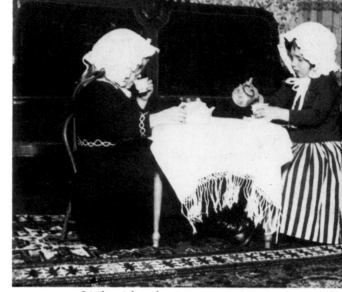

Little girls, playing grown-up, gossip over tea, c.1903.

DATE TRIANGLES

1 cup chopped dates
½ cup sugar
½ cup water
1 teaspoon lemon juice
8 large marshmallows
½ cup butter or margarine,
  softened
1 (3-ounce) package cream
  cheese, softened
2 cups all-purpose flour
¼ teaspoon salt

Combine dates, sugar, water,
lemon juice, and marshmallows
in a medium saucepan; cook
over medium heat, stirring frequently, until marshmallows
melt. Set aside to cool.

Combine butter and cream
cheese in a medium mixing
bowl; beat until smooth. Add
flour and salt; mixing well.
Shape dough into a ball; chill 20
minutes.

Roll pastry to ⅛-inch thickness on a lightly floured surface;
cut into 4-inch squares. Place
one tablespoon date mixture in
center of each square. Moisten
edges of pastry with water; fold

squares in half to form a triangle. Press edges together with a
fork to seal.

Place turnovers on an un-
greased baking sheet. Bake at
400° for 15 minutes or until
lightly browned. Yield: 8 turnovers.

EMPANADAS DULCES

2 cups cooked, mashed sweet
  potatoes
1 (15¼-ounce) can crushed
  pineapple, drained
1¼ cups plus 3 tablespoons
  sugar, divided
1 teaspoon lemon rind
1 teaspoon orange rind
½ teaspoon pumpkin pie
  spice
¼ teaspoon ground cinnamon
2½ cups all-purpose flour
1 teaspoon baking powder
½ teaspoon salt
¾ cup shortening
5 to 6 tablespoons cold water
Additional sugar

Combine sweet potatoes,
pineapple, 1¼ cups sugar,

lemon rind, orange rind, pumpkin pie spice, and cinnamon in
a medium saucepan. Cook over
medium heat, stirring constantly, until thickened. Cool;
set aside.

Combine flour, remaining
sugar, baking powder, and salt
in a medium mixing bowl; cut
in shortening with a pastry
blender until mixture resembles
coarse meal. Sprinkle cold water
evenly over surface; stir with a
fork until dry ingredients are
moistened. Divide pastry into
24 portions. Roll each portion
into a 4-inch cirele on a lightly
floured surface.

Place 1 tablespoon sweet potato mixture in center of each
pastry circle. Moisten edges of
circle; fold pastry in half, making sure edges are even. Using a
fork dipped in flour, press edges
of pastry together to seal.

Sprinkle ½ teaspoon sugar on
each pastry. Place on lightly
greased baking sheets. Bake at
400° for 15 minutes or until
lightly browned. Yield: 2 dozen
turnovers.

BANBURY TARTS

1 cup chopped raisins
1 cup sugar
3 tablespoons graham
  cracker crumbs
1 egg, beaten
Grated rind and juice of 1
  lemon
1 tablespoon butter or
  margarine, melted
⅛ teaspoon salt
Pâté Sucre (page 16)

Combine all ingredients except Pâté Sucre; stir well.

Roll Pâté Sucre to ⅛-inch thickness on a lightly floured surface; cut into 4-inch squares. Place 1 teaspoon raisin mixture in center of each square. Moisten edges with water, and fold pastry in half to form a triangle. Press edges together with a fork to seal.

Place on lightly greased baking sheets. Bake at 425° for 12 minutes or until lightly browned. Yield: 1½ dozen turnovers.

Tea Turnovers (front), Pineapple Pocketbooks and Banbury Tarts.

PINEAPPLE POCKETBOOKS

1 package dry yeast
¼ cup warm water (105°
  to 115°)
6 cups all-purpose flour
1 tablespoon sugar
½ teaspoon salt
2 cups shortening
3 eggs, beaten
1 cup milk
Sugar
Pineapple filling (recipe
  follows)

Dissolve yeast in water; let stand 5 minutes or until bubbly. Set aside.

Combine flour, 1 tablespoon sugar, and salt in a large mixing bowl; mix well. Cut in shortening with a pastry blender until mixture resembles coarse meal. Combine eggs and milk; gradually add to flour mixture, beating at medium speed of electric mixer until smooth. Add yeast mixture, mixing well. Place in a greased bowl, turning to grease top. Cover and let rise in a warm place (85°), free from drafts, 2 hours or until doubled in bulk.

Punch dough down. Sprinkle lightly floured surface with sugar. Roll pastry to ⅛-inch thickness on surface. Cut into thirty 4-inch squares.

Spoon 1 tablespoon pineapple filling in center of each pastry square. Moisten edges of squares; fold pastry in half to form rectangles. Press edges firmly together to seal.

Place on ungreased baking sheets. Bake at 425° for 15 minutes or until lightly browned. Yield: 2½ dozen turnovers.

Pineapple Filling:

1½ cups sugar
3 tablespoons all-purpose
  flour
2⅔ cups crushed pineapple,
  undrained

Combine sugar and flour in a heavy saucepan; blend well. Add pineapple, mixing well. Cook over medium heat, stirring constantly, until sugar dissolves and mixture is thickened. Yield: about 2⅔ cups.

ACKNOWLEDGMENTS

Allison's Little Tea House Coconut Cream Pie, Apricot Tarts, Brown Sugar Tarts, Bourbon-Pumpkin Pie, Sweet Potato-Coconut Pie, Country Apple Pie, Cream Cheese Pastries, Damson Caramel Pie, Osgood Pie, Pineapple-Cottage Cheese Pie, Royal Anne Cherry Pie, Southern Fried Cranberry Pies adapted from *Virginia Cookery, Past and Present* by The Women's Auxiliary of Olivet Episcopal Church, Franconia, Virginia.

Apple Pie Goody courtesy of Mrs. Cheryl Landreth, Pleasant Grove, Alabama.

Apricot Chiffon Pie, Black Walnut Pie adapted from *Julie Benell's Favorite Recipes* by Julie Benell Minor.

Baked Apple Dumplings, Banbury Tarts, Glazed Strawberry Tarts, Lemon Meringue Tarts, Mount Vernon Red Cherry Pie adapted from *Maryland's Way* by Mrs. Lewis R. Andrews and Mrs. J. Reaney Kelly. By permission of the Hammond-Harwood House Association, Annapolis, Maryland.

Bavarian Pie adapted from *The Fredericksburg Home Kitchen Cook Book*, published by The Fredericksburg Home Kitchen Cook Book Central Committee, ©1957.

Blackberry Cobbler, Bourbon Chocolate Pecan Pie, French Silk Chocolate Pie, Loquat Cobbler, Meeting Street Fresh Fig Pie, Pecan Tassies, Pumpkin Chiffon Tarts adapted from *Caterin' To Charleston* by Gloria Mann Maynard, Meredith Maynard Chase, and Holly Maynard Jenkins, ©1981. By permission of Merritt Publishing Co., Charleston, South Carolina.

Blueberry Tarts adapted from *Fascinating Foods from the Deep South* by Alline P. Van Duzor, ©1963. By permission of Crown Publishing Co., New York.

Blue Ribbon Orange Cheesecake, Pineapple Cheesecake adapted from *Flavor Favorites!* by Baylor University Alumni Association, ©1979. By permission of Baylor University Alumni Association, Waco, Texas.

Boiled Apple Dumplings, Ozark Sorghum-Molasses Pie adapted from *Ozarks Cookery* by Eula Mae Stratton, ©1976. By permission of The Ozarks Mountaineer, Branson, Missouri.

Caramel Cream Tarts, Kentucky Apple Cobbler, Lemon Slice Pie adapted from *We Make You Kindly Welcome* by Elizabeth C. Kremer, ©1970. By permission of Shakertown at Pleasant Hill, Harrodsburg, Kentucky.

Cheese Tartlets adapted from *A Source of Much Pleasure*, edited by Virginia Phillips Holtz. By permission of The Mordecai Square Historical Society, Inc., Raleigh, North Carolina.

Chess Meringue, Egg Custard Meringue Pie, Kleeman's Cottage Cheese Pie, Nashville Lemon Pie, Old-Fashioned Caramel Cream Pie, Pecan-Raisin Pie, Pumpkin Meringue Pie adapted from *The Nashville Cookbook*, courtesy of Nashville Area Home Economics Association, Nashville, Tennessee.

Chess Tarts courtesy of Sallie Warner, Nashville, Tennessee.

Chocolate Angel Pie, Wayside Inn Pecan Pie adapted from *Virginia Hospitality* by The Junior League of Hampton Roads, Inc., ©1975. By permission of The Junior League of Hampton Roads, Inc., Newport News, Virginia.

Chocolate Fudge Custard Pie, Fig Streusel Pie adapted from *Prairie Harvest* by St. Peter's Episcopal Churchwomen, Tollville, Arkansas. By permission of St. Peter's Episcopal Churchwomen, Hazen, Arkansas.

Chocolate Icebox Pie, Moonshine Pie, Tyler Pudding Pie adapted from *Recipes from Old Virginia*, compiled by The Virginia Federation of Home Demonstration Clubs, ©1958. By permission of The Virginia Extension Homemakers Council, Austinville, Virginia.

Dewberry Custard Pie by Alice Gann Kaspar and Mocha Cheesecake by Elaine Martini Dove first appeared in *Cook 'Em Horns* by The Ex-Students' Association of The University of Texas, ©1981. By permission of The Ex-Students' Association, The University of Texas, Austin.

Duncan Hines Apple Pie, Old Talbott Tavern Orange Meringue Pie adapted from *Famous Kentucky Recipes*, compiled by The Cabbage Patch Circle, Louisville, Kentucky. By permission of The Cabbage Patch Circle.

Fig Pie, Nesselrode Pie adapted from *The Gasparilla Cookbook*, compiled by The Junior League of Tampa, ©1961. By permission of The Junior League of Tampa, Florida.

Florida Lime Custard Pie, Orange-Cheese Tarts, Mango Pie, Plant City Strawberry Pie, Tupelo Honey Pecan Pie adapted from *Jane Nickerson's Florida Cookbook*, ©1973. By permission of University Presses of Florida, Gainesville.

Georgia Peach Pie, Savannah Christmas Rum Pie adapted from *Savannah Sampler Cookbook* by Margaret Wayt DeBolt, ©1978. By permission of The Donning Company/Publishers, Inc., Norfolk, Virginia.

German Cheesecake, Pecan Chess Pie adapted from *The Mississippi Cookbook*, compiled and edited by the Home Economics Division of the Mississippi Cooperative Extension Service. By permission of University Press of Mississippi, Jackson.

Grandmother's Sweet Potato Cobbler, Oklahoma Bean Pie adapted from *Pioneer Cookery Around Oklahoma*, compiled and edited by Linda Kennedy Rosser, ©1978. By permission of Bobwhite Publications, Oklahoma City, Oklahoma.

Harvest Chiffon Pie, Old Southern Tea Room Lemon Icebox Pie adapted from *The Jackson Cookbook* by Symphony League of Jackson, ©1971. By permission of Symphony League of Jackson, Mississippi.

Hermitage Chess Pie adapted from *By the Board*. Courtesy of The Ladies Hermitage Association.

Hermitage Sweet Potato-Pumpkin Pie, Tennessee Lemon Chess Pie adapted from *The Hermitage Cookbook, Old and New*. Courtesy of The Ladies Hermitage Association, Hermitage, Tennessee.

High Hampton Inn Sunny Silver Pie courtesy of High Hampton Inn and Country Club, Cashiers, North Carolina.

James K. Polk's Vinegar Pie courtesy of Virginia Smartt and Andrena B. Woodward, Nashville, Tennessee.

Ma Ferguson's Pecan Cream Pie adapted from *American Women's Bicentennial Cook Book 1776 - 1976*, ©1975. By permission of Bicentennial Cook Book Corporation, DeSoto, Texas.

Mary's Buttermilk Pie courtesy of Mary Frances Knight, Nashville, Tennessee.

Mincemeat Tarts Flambe, Jennie Selligman's Cream Cheesecake, Marion Flexner's Apple Custard Pie adapted from *Out of Kentucky Kitchens* by Marion Flexner, ©1949. By permission of Franklin Watts, Inc., New York.

Mother's Peach Dumplings courtesy of Mrs. Mac Greer, Mobile, Alabama.

Mrs. Doc's Egg Custard Pie courtesy of Mrs. Doc Cornelius, Guntersville, Alabama.

Old-Fashioned Coconut Custard Pie adapted from *Southern Sideboards*, compiled by The Junior League of Jackson, ©1978. By permission of the Junior League of Jackson, Mississippi.

Peach Cobbler Supreme adapted from *Savannah: Proud As A Peacock* by The Savannah Junior Auxiliary, ©1981. By permission of The Savannah Junior Auxiliary, Savannah, Georgia.

Pecan-Butterscotch Pie, Sour Cream-Raisin Pie, "The Original" Old-Fashioned Cheesecake adapted from *Guten Appetit!* by The Sophienburg Museum, ©1978. By permission of The Sophienburg Memorial Association, New Braunfels, Texas.

Photograph, page 122, from *From the Hills of Georgia, An Autobiography in Paintings* by Mattie Lou O'Kelley, ©1980 by Mattie Lou O'Kelley. Reprinted by permission of Little Brown and Company in association with The Atlantic Monthly.

Pleasant Hill Chocolate Morsel Pie, Rhubarb-Strawberry Cobbler adapted from *Welcome Back to Pleasant Hill* by Elizabeth C. Kremer, ©1977. By permission of Shakertown at Pleasant Hil, Harrodsburg, Kentucky.

Praline Cheesecake adapted from *Favorite Recipes from the Big House* by The N.G. Davis Family, Mobile, Alabama, ©1981. By permission of Cookbook Publishers, Inc., Lenexa, Kansas.

Quote on page 111 from *Eating, Drinking, and Visiting in the South, an Informal History* by Joe Gray Taylor, ©1982. By permission of Louisiana State University Press, Baton Rouge, Louisiana.

Rebecca Boone's Chess Pie courtesy of Audubon State Park, Henderson, Arkansas.

Sherry Tarts adapted from *Charleston Receipts*, collected by The Junior League of Charleston, ©1950. By permission of The Junior League of Charleston, South Carolina.

Smith and Welton's Tea Room Butterscotch Meringue Pie courtesy of Smith and Welton's Tea Room, Norfolk.

Sugar Pies courtesy of Mrs. Clint Wyrick, Garland, Texas.

Virginia Holiday Cream Pie adapted from *Plantation Recipes* by Lessie Bowers, ©1959. By permission of Robert Speller and Sons, New York.

Virginia Pumpkin Pie courtesy of Mrs. Edna Traccarella, Fairfax, Virginia.

Weidmann's Bourbon Pie, Weidmann's Sherry Chiffon Pie courtesy of Weidmann's Restaurant, Meridian, Mississippi.

Self-sealing Pie Tins.

PATENTED.

Tin Containing Pie Ready for Baking.

Separate Parts.

INDEX

Almond Cream Pie, Coffee-, 93
Apples
  Apple-Cranberry Pie with Cheese
    Pastry, 32
  Apple-Pecan Pie, 29
  Apple Pie Goody, 32
  Cobbler, Kentucky Apple, 33
  Country Apple Pie, 29
  Crumb-Topped Apple Pie, 31
  Custard Pie, Marion Flexner's
    Apple, 69
  Dumplings, Baked Apple, 128
  Dumplings, Boiled Apple, 129
  Duncan Hines Apple Pie, 28
  Fried Apple Pies, 132
  Pot Pie, Apple, 33
  Praline-Topped Apple Pie, 30
  Skillet Apple Pie, Travellers'
    Rest, 31
Applesauce Turnovers, 135
Apricots
  Chiffon Pie, Apricot, 109
  Fried Apricot Pies, 132
  Tarts, Apricot, 116

Banana Cream Pie, Kentucky, 93
Banbury Tarts, 137
Basic Pastry How-To, 14-15
Bavarian Pie, 104
Bean Pie, Oklahoma, 57
Berry Cobbler, 47
Berry Pie, 47
Blackberries
  Berry Pie, 47
  Cobbler, Berry, 47
  Cobbler, Deep-Dish
    Blackberry, 48
  Dumplings, Blackberry, 130
Black Bottom Pie, Delta, 105
Black Walnut Pie, 55
Blueberries
  Berry Pie, 47
  Cobbler, Berry, 47
  Cobbler Roll, Blueberry, 47
  Huckleberry Pie, 47
  Tarts, Blueberry, 116
Bourbon Pie, Weidmann's, 113
Bourbon Chocolate Pecan Pie, 54
Bourbon-Pumpkin Pie, 62

Bourbon Sauce, 44
Brown Sugar Chess Pie, 73
Brown Sugar Tarts, 119
Buttermilk Cream Pie, 88
Buttermilk Pie, German, 67
Buttermilk Pie, Mary's, 66
Butterscotch
  Pecan-Butterscotch Pie, 101
  Smith and Welton's Tea Room
    Butterscotch Meringue Pie, 90

Caramel
  Cream Pie, Old-Fashioned
    Caramel, 91
  Damson Caramel Pie, 75
  Tarts, Caramel Cream, 119
Cheese Pastry, Cheddar, 16
Cheese Pastry, Double-Crust, 32
Cheese Pies and Cheesecakes
  Cottage Cheese Pie,
    Kleeman's, 78
  Cream Cheesecake, Jennie
    Selligman's, 80
  German Cheesecake, 81
  Mocha Cheesecake, 79
  Old-Fashioned Cheesecake,
    "The Original," 78
  Orange Cheesecake, Blue
    Ribbon, 82
  Pineapple Cheesecake, 83
  Pineapple-Cottage Cheese
    Pie, 82
  Praline Cheesecake, 84
  Pumpkin Cheesecake, 85
  Tartlets, Cheese, 122
  Tarts, Orange-Cheese, 118
Cherries
  Cream Pie, Coconut-Cherry, 94
  Red Cherry Pie, Mount
    Vernon, 34
  Royal Anne Cherry Pie, 35
  Tarts, Petite Cherry, 121
Chess Pies
  Brown Sugar Chess Pie, 73
  Caramel Pie, Damson, 75
  Chocolate Chess Pie, 73
  Hermitage Chess Pie, 72

Lemon Chess Pie, Tennessee, 74
Lemon Pie, Nashville, 76
Meringue Pie, Chess, 73
Orange Pie, Lee Family, 76
Osgood Pie, 77
Pecan Chess Pie, 74
Pudding Pie, Tyler, 75
Rebecca Boone's Chess Pie, 72
Sorghum-Molasses Pie,
  Ozark, 77
Tarts, Chess, 119
Transparent Pie, Telfair, 75
Vinegar Pie, James K. Polk's, 77
Chiffon Pies. See Refrigerated Pies.
Chocolate
  Angel Pie, Chocolate, 92
  Black Bottom Pie, Delta, 105
  Bourbon Chocolate Pecan
    Pie, 54
  Chess Pie, Chocolate, 73
  Chocolate Morsel Pie, Pleasant
    Hill, 68
  Cream Pie, Chocolate, 92
  Cream Pie, Chocolate Rum, 104
  French Huguenot Chocolate
    Pie, 68
  French Silk Chocolate Pie, 112
  Fudge Pie, Chocolate Lover's, 67
  Fudge Pie, No-Crust, 68
  Icebox Pie, Chocolate, 112
  Meringue Pie, Chocolate, 91
  Mocha Cheesecake, 79
  Pecan Pie, Chocolate, 53
  Piecrust, Chocolate Crumb, 104
  Piecrust, Chocolate Wafer, 22
Cobblers
  Apple Cobbler, Kentucky, 33
  Berry Cobbler, 47
  Blackberry Cobbler,
    Deep-Dish, 48
  Blueberry Cobbler Roll, 47
  Fig Cobbler, Fresh, 36
  Grape Cobbler, Green, 37
  Loquat Cobbler, 38
  Peach Cobbler, Easy, 40
  Peach Cobbler Supreme, 40
  Rhubarb-Strawberry Cobbler, 43
  Sweet Potato Cobbler,
    Grandmother's, 58

Coconut
 Cream Pie, Allison's Little Tea
  House Coconut, 94
 Cream Pie, Coconut-Cherry, 94
 Cream Pie,
  Coconut-Pineapple, 95
 Cream Pie, Fresh Coconut, 96
 Custard Pie, Old-Fashioned
  Coconut, 71
 Meringue Pie, Coconut, 95
 Piecrust, Coconut, 23
 Piecrust, Coconut-Graham, 21
 Sweet Potato-Coconut Pie, 58
Coffee-Almond Cream Pie, 93
Cranberries
 Apple-Cranberry Pie with Cheese
  Pastry, 32
 Cranberry Pie, 48
 Fried Cranberry Pies,
  Southern, 134
Cream Cheese Pastries, 135
Cream Cheese Pastry, 123
Cream Cheese Pastry Shell, 20
Cream Pies
 Banana Cream Pie,
  Kentucky, 93
 Buttermilk Cream Pie, 88
 Butterscotch Meringue Pie,
  Smith and Welton's Tea
  Room, 90
 Caramel Cream Pie,
  Old-Fashioned, 91
 Chocolate Angel Pie, 92
 Chocolate Cream Pie, 92
 Chocolate Meringue Pie, 91
 Chocolate Rum Cream Pie, 104
 Coconut-Cherry Cream Pie, 94
 Coconut Cream Pie, Allison's
  Little Tea House, 94
 Coconut Cream Pie, Fresh, 96
 Coconut Meringue Pie, 95
 Coconut-Pineapple Cream
  Pie, 95
 Coffee-Almond Cream Pie, 93
 Festive Cream Pie, 101
 Grape Juice Pie, 96
 Jeff Davis Pie, 89
 Lemon Meringue Pie, 98
 Lemon Pie, Heavenly, 96
 Lime Pie, Florida, 98
 Moonshine Pie, 90
 Orange Meringue Pie, 100
 Orange Meringue Pie, Old
  Talbott Tavern, 99
 Peanut Cream Pie, Crunchy, 96
 Pecan-Butterscotch Pie, 101
 Pecan Cream Pie, Ma
  Ferguson's, 100
 Vanilla Cream Pie, 88
 Virginia Holiday Cream Pie, 89
Custard Pies
 Apple Custard Pie, Marion
  Flexner's, 69
 Buttermilk Pie, German, 67
 Buttermilk Pie, Mary's, 68
 Chocolate Morsel Pie, Pleasant
  Hill, 68
 Chocolate Pie, French
  Huguenot, 68

Coconut Custard Pie,
 Old-Fashioned, 71
Dewberry Custard Pie, 70
Egg Custard Meringue Pie, 67
Egg Custard Pie, Mrs. Doc's, 67
Fudge Pie, Chocolate
 Lover's, 67
Fudge Pie, No-Crust, 68
Lime Custard Pie, Florida, 70
Sour Cream-Raisin Pie, 70

Damson Caramel Pie, 75
Dates
 Tarts, Miniature
  Date-Pecan, 124
 Triangles, Date, 136
Delta Black Bottom Pie, 105
Dewberry Custard Pie, 70
Dumplings
 Apple Dumplings, Baked, 128
 Apple Dumplings, Boiled, 129
 Blackberry Dumplings, 130
 Peach Dumplings,
  Mother's, 130

Eggnog Pie, 106
Egg Pastry Shells, 20
Empanadas Dulces, 136

Festive Cream Pie, 101
Figs
 Cobbler, Fresh Fig, 36
 Fig Pie, 35
 Fresh Fig Pie, Meeting
  Street, 109
 Streusel Pie, Fig, 35
Filbert-Graham Piecrust, 21
Filling, Pineapple, 137
Fried Pies. See also Turnovers.
 Apple Pies, Fried, 132
 Apricot Pies, Fried, 132
 Cranberry Pies, Southern
  Fried, 134
 Peach Pies, Fried, 134
Fruit Pies
 Apple Cobbler, Kentucky, 33
 Apple-Cranberry Pie with Cheese
  Pastry, 32
 Apple-Pecan Pie, 29
 Apple Pie, Country, 29
 Apple Pie, Crumb-Topped, 31
 Apple Pie, Duncan Hines, 28
 Apple Pie Goody, 32
 Apple Pie, Praline-Topped, 30
 Apple Pie, Travellers' Rest
  Skillet, 31
 Apple Pot Pie, 33
 Cherry Pie, Mount Vernon
  Red, 34
 Cherry Pie, Royal Anne, 35
 Fig Cobbler, Fresh, 36
 Fig Pie, 35
 Fig Streusel Pie, 35
 Grape Cobbler, Green, 37
 Lemon Slice Pie, 37
 Loquat Cobbler, 38
 Mango Pie, 38
 Mincemeat, Mrs. Fitzhugh
  Lee's, 44

Mincemeat Pie with Bourbon
 Sauce, 44
Muscadine Pie, 36
Peach Cobbler, Easy, 40
Peach Cobbler Supreme, 40
Peach Meringue Pie, Fresh, 39
Peach Pie, Georgia, 39
Peach Pie, Glazed, 40
Pear Crumble Pie, 41
Pear Mincemeat Pie, 41
Pear Pie, Old-Fashioned, 41
Persimmon Pie, 42
Plum Meringue Pie, 42
Raisin Pie, 44
Rhubarb Pie, 43
Rhubarb-Strawberry Cobbler, 43
Fudge Pie, Chocolate Lover's, 67
Fudge Pie, No-Crust, 68

Gingersnap Piecrust, 22
Graham
 Piecrust, Coconut-Graham, 21
 Piecrust, Filbert-Graham, 21
 Piecrust, Graham Cracker, 21
Grape Cobbler, Green, 37
Grape Juice Pie, 96

High Hampton Inn Sunny Silver
 Pie, 106
Honey Pecan Pie, Tupelo, 52
Huckleberry Pie, 47

Icebox Pies. See Refrigerated Pies.

Jeff Davis Pie, 89

Lemon
 Chess Pie, Tennessee Lemon, 74
 Chiffon Pie, Tart Lemon, 107
 Icebox Pie, Old Southern Tea
  Room Lemon, 113
 Lemon Pie, Heavenly, 96
 Lemon Pie, Nashville, 76
 Lemon Slice Pie, 37
 Meringue Pie, Lemon, 98
 Tarts, Dainty Lemon, 125
 Tarts, Lemon, 118
 Tarts, Lemon Chiffon, 118
 Tarts, Lemon Meringue, 117
Lime
 Custard Pie, Florida Lime, 70
 Florida Lime Pie, 98
 Key Lime Pie, Florida, 112
 Luscious Lime Pie, 107
 Tarts, Lime Chiffon, 118
Loquat Cobbler, 38

Maids of Honor, 120
Mango Pie, 38
Meringue Pie Shell, 92
Meringue Toppings
 Basic Meringue, 24
 Basic Meringue How-To, 24
 Pineapple Meringue, 25
 Powdered Sugar Meringue, 25
 Unbaked Meringue, 25

Mincemeat
  Bourbon Sauce, Mincemeat Pie
    with, 44
  Mrs. Fitzhugh Lee's
    Mincemeat, 44
  Pear Mincemeat Pie, 41
  Tarts Flambe, Mincemeat, 120
Mocha Cheesecake, 79
Molasses Pie, Ozark Sorghum-, 77
Moonshine Pie, 90
Muscadine Pie, 36
Nesselrode Pie, 108

Nuts. See specific types.

Oranges
  Cheesecake, Blue Ribbon
    Orange, 82
  Lee Family Orange Pie, 76
  Meringue Pie, Old Talbott Tavern
    Orange, 99
  Meringue Pie, Orange, 100
  Tarts, Orange-Cheese, 118
Osgood Pie, 77

Pastries and Piecrusts
  Basic Pastry, 14
  Butter Pastry, Basic, 12
  Cheese Pastry, Cheddar, 16
  Cheese Pastry, Double-Crust, 32
  Chocolate Crumb Piecrust, 104
  Chocolate Wafer Piecrust, 22
  Coconut-Graham Piecrust, 21
  Coconut Piecrust, 23
  Corn Flake Piecrust, 23
  Cream Cheese Pastries, 135
  Cream Cheese Pastry, 123
  Cream Cheese Pastry Shell, 20
  Deep-Dish Pastry, 16
  Double-Crust Pastry, Basic, 12
  Egg Pastry Shells, 20
  Filbert-Graham Piecrust, 21
  Gingersnap Piecrust, 22
  Graham Cracker Piecrust, 21
  Lard Pastry, Best, 12
  Lattice-Top Pastry, 12, 43
  Meringue Pie Shell, 92
  Mix, Pastry, 12
  Pâte Brisée Sucrée, 16
  Pecan Pastry Shell, 20
  Puff Paste, 18
  Quantity Pastry, 12
  "Short" Pastry, 12
  Single-Crust Pastry Shell, 12
  Stir 'n' Roll Pastry Shell, Dr.
    David Wesson's, 17
  Tart Shells, 125
  Tart Shells, All-Purpose, 20
  Vanilla Wafer Piecrust, 22
  Zwieback Piecrust, 23
Pâte Brisée Sucrée, 16
Peaches
  Cobbler, Easy Peach, 40
  Cobbler Supreme, Peach, 40
  Dumplings, Mother's Peach, 130
  Fried Peach Pies, 134
  Georgia Peach Pie, 39
  Glazed Peach Pie, 40

Meringue Pie, Fresh Peach, 39
  Tartlets, Peach, 122
Peanuts
  Cream Pie, Crunchy Peanut, 96
  Peanut Brittle Pie, 113
  Peanut Pie, 52
Pears
  Old-Fashioned Pear Pie, 41
  Pear Crumble Pie, 41
  Pear Mincemeat Pie, 41
Pecans
  Alabama Pecan Pie, 52
  Apple-Pecan Pie, 29
  Bourbon Chocolate Pecan
    Pie, 54
  Butterscotch Pie, Pecan-, 101
  Chess Pie, Pecan, 74
  Chocolate Pecan Pie, 53
  Cream Pie, Ma Ferguson's
    Pecan, 100
  Pastry Shell, Pecan, 20
  Pumpkin-Pecan Pie, 61
  Raisin Pie, Pecan-, 54
  Sweet Potato-Pecan Pie,
    Virginia, 58
  Tarts, Miniature
    Date-Pecan, 124
  Tassies, Pecan, 124
  Texas Pecan Pie, 52
  Texas Poor Boy Pie, 55
  Tupelo Honey Pecan Pie, 52
  Wayside Inn Pecan Pie, 53
Persimmon Pie, 42
Pineapple
  Cheesecake, Pineapple, 83
  Cream Pie,
    Coconut-Pineapple, 95
  Filling, Pineapple, 137
  Meringue, Pineapple, 25
  Pineapple-Cottage Cheese Pie, 82
  Pineapple Pocketbooks, 137
Plum Meringue Pie, 42
Potato Pie, Maryland White, 57
Praline Cheesecake, 84
Praline-Topped Apple Pie, 30
Pudding Pie, Tyler, 75
Puff Paste, 18
Pumpkin
  Bourbon-Pumpkin Pie, 62
  Cheesecake, Pumpkin, 85
  Chiffon Pie, Pumpkin, 111
  Meringue Pie, Pumpkin, 61
  Pecan Pie, Pumpkin-, 61
  Sweet Potato-Pumpkin Pie,
    Hermitage, 59
  Tarts, Pumpkin Chiffon, 118
  Virginia Pumpkin Pie, 61

Raisins
  Pecan-Raisin Pie, 54
  Raisin Pie, 44
  Sour Cream-Raisin Pie, 70
Raspberries
  Berry Pie, 47
  Cobbler, Berry, 47
  Raspberry Pie, 49
Refrigerated Pies
  Apricot Chiffon Pie, 109
  Bavarian Pie, 104

Black Bottom Pie, Delta, 105
  Bourbon Pie, Weidmann's, 113
  Chocolate Icebox Pie, 112
  Chocolate Pie, French Silk, 112
  Chocolate Rum Cream Pie, 104
  Eggnog Pie, 106
  Fig Pie, Meeting Street
    Fresh, 109
  Key Lime Pie, Florida, 112
  Lemon Chiffon Pie, Tart, 107
  Lemon Icebox Pie, Old Southern
    Tea Room, 113
  Lime Pie, Luscious, 107
  Nesselrode Pie, 108
  Peanut Brittle Pie, 113
  Pumpkin Chiffon Pie, 111
  Rum Pie, Savannah
    Christmas, 108
  Sherry Chiffon Pie,
    Weidmann's, 109
  Sunny Silver Pie, High Hampton
    Inn, 106
  Sweet Potato Chiffon Pie, 111
  Vanilla Chiffon Pie, 104
Rhubarb Pie, 43
Rhubarb-Strawberry Cobbler, 43

Sauce, Bourbon, 44
Sherry Chiffon Pie,
  Weidmann's, 109
Sherry Tarts, 120
Silver Pie, High Hampton Inn
  Sunny, 106
Sorghum-Molasses Pie, Ozark, 77
Squash
  Butternut Squash Pie, 63
  Yellow Squash Pie, 63
Strawberry Cobbler, Rhubarb-, 43
Strawberry Pie, Plant City, 49
Strawberry Tarts, Glazed, 117
Sugar Pies, 135
Sweet Potatoes
  Chiffon Pie, Sweet Potato, 111
  Cobbler, Grandmother's Sweet
    Potato, 58
  Coconut Pie, Sweet Potato-, 58
  1894 Sweet Potato Pie, 57
  Empanadas Dulces, 136
  Hermitage Sweet
    Potato-Pumpkin Pie, 59
  Mary Randolph's Sweet Potato
    Pie, 57
  Pecan Pie, Virginia Sweet
    Potato-, 58

Tarts
  Apricot Tarts, 116
  Banbury Tarts, 137
  Blueberry Tarts, 116
  Brown Sugar Tarts, 119
  Caramel Cream Tarts, 119
  Cheese Tartlets, 122
  Cherry Tarts, Petite, 121
  Chess Tarts, 119
  Date-Pecan Tarts,
    Miniature, 124
  Lemon Chiffon Tarts 118
  Lemon Meringue Tarts, 117
  Lemon Tarts, 118

Tarts, *(continued)*
  Lemon Tarts, Dainty, 125
  Lime Chiffon Tarts, 118
  Maids of Honor, 120
  Martha White's Teatime
    Tassies, 123
  Mincemeat Tarts Flambe, 120
  Orange-Cheese Tarts, 118
  Peach Tartlets, 122
  Pecan Tassies, 124
  Pumpkin Chiffon Tarts, 118
  Shells, All-Purpose Tart, 20
  Shells, Tart, 125
  Sherry Tarts, 120
  Strawberry Tarts, Glazed, 117
Texas Poor Boy Pie, 55
Transparent Pie, Telfair, 75
Tomato Pie, Green, 63
Turnovers
  Applesauce Turnovers, 135

  Banbury Tarts, 137
  Cream Cheese Pastries, 135
  Date Triangles, 136
  Empanadas Dulces, 136
  Pâté Sucre, 16
  Pineapple Pocketbooks, 137
  Sugar Pies, 135
  Tea Turnovers, 136
Tyler Pudding Pie, 75

Vanilla Chiffon Pie, 104
Vanilla Cream Pie, 88
Vanilla Wafer Piecrust, 22
Vegetable Pies
  Bean Pie, Oklahoma, 57
  Potato Pie, Maryland White, 57
  Pumpkin Chiffon Pie, 111
  Pumpkin Meringue Pie, 61
  Pumpkin-Pecan Pie, 61
  Pumpkin Pie, Bourbon-, 62

Pumpkin Pie, Virginia, 61
Squash Pie, Butternut, 63
Squash Pie, Yellow, 63
Sweet Potato Chiffon Pie, 111
Sweet Potato Cobbler,
  Grandmother's, 58
Sweet Potato-Coconut Pie, 58
Sweet Potato-Pecan Pie,
  Virginia, 58
Sweet Potato Pie, 1894, 57
Sweet Potato Pie, Mary
  Randolph's, 57
Sweet Potato-Pumpkin Pie,
  Hermitage, 59
Tomato Pie, Green, 63
Vinegar Pie, James K. Polk's 77
Virginia Holiday Cream Pie, 89

Walnut Pie, Black, 55

Zwieback Piecrust, 23

Simple Simon met a pieman
    Going to the fair;
Said Simple Simon to the pieman,
    "Let me taste your ware."

Said the pieman to Simple Simon,
    "Show me first your penny."
Said Simple Simon to the pieman,
    "Indeed, I have not any."